Thomas S. Hill

The Registers of the Parish of Thorington in the County of Suffolk

Thomas S. Hill

The Registers of the Parish of Thorington in the County of Suffolk

ISBN/EAN: 9783337154493

Printed in Europe, USA, Canada, Australia, Japan

Cover: Foto ©ninafisch / pixelio.de

More available books at **www.hansebooks.com**

The Registers

OF THE

PARISH OF THORINGTON

IN THE COUNTY OF SUFFOLK.

This View of Thorington Church is copied from
a Volume of Drawings of Suffolk Churches,
made by Isaac Johnson of Woodbridge, between
1793 and 1816.

The Registers

OF THE

Parish of Thorington

IN THE COUNTY OF SUFFOLK,

WITH

NOTES OF THE DIFFERENT ACTS OF PARLIAMENT REFERRING
TO THEM,

AND

NOTICES OF THE BENCE FAMILY, WITH PEDIGREE,

AND OTHER FAMILIES WHOSE NAMES APPEAR THEREIN.

EDITED BY

THOMAS S. HILL, B.C.L., M.A.,

RECTOR OF THORINGTON.

LONDON:
MITCHELL AND HUGHES, 140 WARDOUR STREET, W.
1884.

PREFACE.

In editing these Registers I have added such items of information as I could gather relating to the families of those whose names occur therein, and also regarding the different Acts of Parliament by which entries in Registers have been affected, so as to give the book more historical interest. One of the chief motives that induced me to undertake the task of putting the Registers into print was a desire that the inhabitants of the parish should be able, if they wished, to feel more personal interest in it and the families that have resided here. In these days people very easily forget that the same work has been going on, the same houses occupied, the same relative duties fulfilled by former generations, who were of just as much importance and as necessary to fulfil them as those who are fulfilling them now.

By the kindness of the Bence Family I give a very full statement of their pedigree. They have been an influential family in this neighbourhood for more than three hundred years, dating their recorded history from the time when they were the most important of the inhabitants of Aldborough, and have held the chief portion of the property in this parish since 1691, when they bought the estate of the Coke Family, who were the previous owners. In that portion of their pedigree relating to the Rev. Thomas Bence, Rector of Kelsale-cum-Carlton, who died 1757, the descendants of Catherine, who married Gabriel Trusson, and whose daughter Catherine married Anthony Collet, are represented now by the Rev. Anthony Collett, Rector of Hastingleigh in Kent.

I am able also, by the kindness of F. A. Crisp, Esq., to give a photo-lithographic copy of an old engraving of Thorington Church, copied from a volume of drawings of Suffolk Churches made by Isaac Johnson of Woodbridge between 1793 and 1816.

I thought it of interest also to give the names of the Rectors of the parish, and, as I have stated elsewhere, Dr. Bensly, the Diocesan Registrar, has enabled me, at much inconvenience and trouble to himself, to give a complete list of all the Rectors from December 1331, the date of the first recorded institution, to the present day, by which I learn that

I am the fifty-third recorded Rector in direct succession from the institution of Jo'es Fowas de Donewyco. The Priory of Blythburgh held the patronage of the church and rectory before this date, as in their charter, dated in the last year of Richard I., the gift of the advowson and of land in the parish to the Priory by William, son of Walter de Sadenfield is referred to. I have, however, in my possession an old Chartulary of the Priory in which this gift is mentioned as having been made by Galfride de Beletone, and afterward confirmed by William de Sadenfield. Fourteen pages of this Chartulary relate to Thorington, and a copy of the first page, which contains the record of this gift of Galfride de Beletone, I have had taken by photo-lithographic process by Mr. Griggs of Peckham, and have added it to this book. The Historical Manuscripts Commission of the Rolls House have examined this Chartulary, and will give a notice of it in the Report they present to Parliament next year. The Rectors from the date of this gift to the institution of Jo'es Fowas are not recorded in the books of the Diocesan Registry, and, as the tower and walls of the body of the church are of Early Norman date, it seems tolerably certain that the fabric has been in existence at least since 1130, so that two hundred years of the early ecclesiastical history of the parish leave no traces of the Rectors that officiated here.

The Registers of this parish are not the only Suffolk Registers that are published. Those of Tannington and Ellough have already been printed, and those of Brundish and Carlton (by Kelsale) are in the printers' hands, and I think that increased interest in the past history of our parishes would be encouraged by a wider publication of these records.

I have added an Appendix of names entered since 1882, for I have taken longer time in publishing the book than I anticipated, and the type, after a sufficient number of copies had been printed, was broken up. I have brought the entries down to the latest possible date.

THOMAS S. HILL.

THORINGTON RECTORY,

    October 1884.

Sciant p̃ et f̃ q̃ ego Ga
id B̃. Bacchie ẽcc̃ie sc̃ ꝼxpi
De meo i villa de Thartone
rius pat̃onat̃ sc̃ ecc̃ie p̃i
p̃o ob̃tuer̃ et ĩ fã ꝗm asnce
ꝗ omune vñã · a bd austj̃
me et hẽpo meo li · et q̃ · p̃asi
hẽpo mei ẽxanticabimỹ se
vñã au abuocatõe scã ecc̃
hõies et fe · rus̃os et frãnos

Sciant p̃ et f̃ · q̃ ego Wille
so et ecc̃ie sc̃ mꝑie ?
ego spẽbit au p̃uñcꝼ que iac
au abnocatõe eis · ecc̃ie se
capã suã i̅de ofecñã plenꝓ
et cui̅ habeãnt et teneãnt p̃
au p̃uñcꝼ ꝗetãe et solicꝼ ab ·
cafte mee ꝗsimac̃ foa · p s
ahẽpo mei ẽxauntõ et sẽfeñ
ptone au p̃au scã ecc̃io ·
fi · pu et ipe · de · mea · ꝼuai

Sciant p̃ et f̃ · q̃ ego Ell
et ecc̃io scã mꝑio se
ego spẽbit au p̃uñcꝼ ꝗ iac̃
cañe eis · ecc̃ie se Thanc̃
fctã plenꝓ auestãti et oco
Thartõn suaꝓ volo et oco

I am the fifty-third recorded Rector in direct succession from the institution of Jo'es Fowas de Donewyco. The Priory of Blythburgh held the patronage of the church and rectory before this date, as in their charter, dated in the last year of Richard I., the gift of the advowson and of land in the parish to the Priory by William, son of Walter de Sadenfield is referred to. I have, however, in my possession an old Chartulary of the Priory in which this gift is mentioned as having been made by Galfride de Beletone, and afterward confirmed by William de Sadenfield. Fourteen pages of this Chartulary relate to Thorington, and a copy of the first page, which contains the record of this gift of Galfride de Beletone, I have had taken by photo-lithographic process by Mr. Griggs of Peckham, and have added it to this book. The Historical Manuscripts Commission of the Rolls House have examined this Chartulary, and will give a notice of it in the Report they present to Parliament next year. The Rectors from the date of this gift to the institution of Jo'es Fowas are not recorded in the books of the Diocesan Registry, and, as the tower and walls of the body of the church are of Early Norman date, it seems tolerably certain that the fabric has been in existence at least since 1130, so that two hundred years of the early ecclesiastical history of the parish leave no traces of the Rectors that officiated here.

The Registers of this parish are not the only Suffolk Registers that are published. Those of Tannington and Ellough have already been printed, and those of Brundish and Carlton (by Kelsale) are in the printers' hands, and I think that increased interest in the past history of our parishes would be encouraged by a wider publication of these records.

I have added an Appendix of names entered since 1882, for I have taken longer time in publishing the book than I anticipated, and the type, after a sufficient number of copies had been printed, was broken up. I have brought the entries down to the latest possible date.

THOMAS S. HILL.

THORINGTON RECTORY,

October 1884.

אמנאל

(Incorrectly for עמנואל—Emmanuel.)

REGESTUM THORINGTONIÆ.

ROBERT' GOLDE,

Rector eiusdem

Oppiduli.

NOTICES

OF THE

Parish Church of Thorington,

Suffolk.

———◆———

RECTORS OF THORINGTON.

On the inside of the cover and on the first page of the First Register Book there is a list of Rectors from the year 1593 to the present time, with the exception of Samuel Ledys, 1610-12 ; but as by the kindness of W. T. Bensly, Esq., LL.D., Deputy-Registrar of the Diocese, I am able to give a correct list of all the Rectors from the first recorded Institution in 1332, I prefer giving this completed list to merely copying those in the Thorington Register Book. To Dr. Bensly's courtesy the completeness and correctness of this list of Rectors is entirely due. Free access to the Institution Books and unlimited time for examination was liberally allowed me, and the list when completed received his supervision and corrections.

This list is taken from Tanner's MS. in the Norwich Diocesan Registry, down to the institution of Robert Smith, A.D. 1484, and compared with the entries made in the Institution Books in the same Registry, from which quotations, when made, are inserted in brackets. After the institution of Robert Smith, where the list in Tanner's MS. terminates, all the extracts are made from the Institution Books, which commence A.D. 1299.

The 'Tanner's MS.' or 'Norwich Domesday Book' which is here referred to, is a large folio volume of nearly a thousand pages, written in Latin, in modern Gothic character. It is a survey of all the parishes of the Diocese of Norwich with the temporalities and spiritualities of the Priors and Monks and other religious houses in the several parishes. It gives an account of all the livings in the Diocese, procurations, synodals, and other payments, at some unstated date ; but internal evidence proves that it commenced about the beginning of and continued nearly to the end of the fifteenth century.—*Vide* First Report of the Historical MSS. Commission, 1870, page 87.

[*The bequest of Rob. Hoo, dated 1503, implies that its continuation entered on the sixteenth century.*—T. S. H.]

One omission of Institution, when Francis Kynaston became Rector, will be noticed A.D. 1620, but this omission is rectified by the Register Book of this Parish, where "Francis Kynnaston, Rector Ecclesiae de Thorington," is "writ large." The omission is supposed to have arisen from the confusion consequent on Bishop Jegon's death in 1617 and his successor's, Bishop Overall, in 1619, for the Institution Books are for four or five years at that time not accurately kept.

To Colonel Chester, LL.D., Editor of the 'Westminster Abbey Registers,' I am indebted for the University status of most of the later Rectors.

Instead of placing notes at the bottom of the page I insert them in Italics immediately following the passages referred to.

TANNER'S MS.

968.   d. d. s. Petro [B. 299, vi. 214.
                 Thoryton [ii.]   Thuryton [v.]
            Thorington [ii. iv.]   Tharington [vii., viii.]

Domesd.   Prior de Blyburgh habet cam' in proprios usus. Vicarius habet mansum pertinens Eccl'iæ cum xv. acris terræ, estimatur ad viij marc. integr. Procuratio vj⁹ viij⁴. vicarius solvit Synodalia per cotum an'um xij⁴. Denarij S. Petri iiij ob.

Books of Institution.	Dates.	Rectors.	Patrons.
Lib. ii. 51.	xi. Kal. Jan. 1332.	Jo'es Fowas de Donewyco. [Vndecimo Kalen' Januar' Anno et loco p'd'cis [*the prior institution was "apud Cantebriq'"*] Joh'es ffowas de Donewico p'sbit' institut' fuit cano'e p' p'd'car vicariu' in eccl'ia de Thory'ton vacante. ad p'sentaco'em relig' viror' P'oris et cano'icor' eccl'ie b'e marie de Blybourgh' veror' eiusdem eccl'ie patronor'. Lib. Instit.]	Prior et Canon. de Blyburgh.
„ „ 68.	Id. Nov. 1331.	Phil. de Berton de Stowemercato.	....
Lib. iii. 60.	24 July 1342.	Rog. de Whatecroft de P. Jernemutà. [*Yarmouth.*] [p. mut cum Stowmercat. per liberam resignacionem Philippi de Berton. Lib. Instit.]	....
Lib. iv. 115.	14 Nov. 1349.	Will. de Snitterton. [Willi'us de Suyt'ton. Lib. Instit.]	....
„ „ 155.	10 Dec. 1354.	Warinus Martel. [per liberam resignacionem Willi' de Snet'ton. Lib. Instit.]	....
Lib. v. 50.	15 Sep. 1361.	Tho. de Honyngham.	....
„ „ 71.	27 Oct. 1366.	Rob. Cole. [p. mut. cum S. Sim. et Jud. de Norw. per liberam resignacionem Thome de Honyngham ultimi Rectoris. Lib. Instit.]	....

Books of Institution.	Dates.	Rectors.	Patrons.
.... 80.	1 Mart. 1367.	Jo'es Bonore.	....
	[p. mnt. cum lib. cap. in Palatio Dⁿⁱ London Epi. per liberam resignacionem Robti. Cole ultimi Rectoris. Lib. Instit.]		
Lib. vi. 46.	pen. Julij, 1376.	Rob. Hierd de Colne Engayne.	....
„ „ 123.	11 Jul. 1387.	Walt. Styrop de Thouiston.	....
„ „ 214.	21 Jul. 1396.	Jo'es Edward.	....
„ „ 248.	alt. Jul. 1399.	Rob. Ovy.	....
Lib. vii. 41.	23 Jun. 1411.	Jo'es Cory de Lyng.	....
	[per liberam resignacionem Robti. Ovy ultimi Rectoris. Lib. Instit.]		
„ „ 85.	7 Nov. 1414.	Tho. Frenge de Walsyngham.	....
	[de Walsingham Magna .... per liberam resignacionem Johannis Cory de Lyng ultimi Rectoris. Lib. Instit.]		
Lib. viii. 40.	6 Jan. 1418.	Will. Sandyacre.	....
	p. mnt. cum Basyngham. [Willi'us Sandyacre (Rector de Basyngham) per liberam resignacionem Thome Frenge de Walsyngham Magna. Lib. Instit.]		
„ „ 48.	6 Nov. 1419.	Tho. Smyth.	....
		Tho. Dysse.	
Lib. ix. 88.	8 Nov. 1436.	Rob. Wode.	....
	[per liberam resignacionem Thome Dysse. Lib. Instit.] See Monumental Inscriptions.		
Lib. xi. 123.	17 Jan. 1460.	Walt. Hunne.	....
	[per mortem Roberti Wode. Lib. Instit.]		
„ „ 139.	pen. Jan. 1463.	Mich. Gosse.	....
	[per liberam resignacionem Walteri Hunne. Lib. Instit.]		
„ „ 142.	22 Jun. 1464.	Tho. Medewe.	....
	[per liberam resignacionem Mich'is Gosse niti' Rect'. Lib. Instit.]		
„ „ 153.	26 Mart. 1466.	Ric. Gorston.	....
		Rad. Croston.	
„ „ 166.	23 Mart. 1467.	Will. Thure.	....
	[per mortem Radulphi Croston ultimi Rectoris. Lib. Instit.]		
Lib. xii. 62.	9 Jul. 1478.	Ric. Marshall.	....
	[Ricardus Marshale ...... per liberam resignacionem Will'mi Thure. Lib. Instit.]		
„ „ 110.	12 Oct. 1484.	Rob. Smith,	....
	Rob'tus Smyth .... per liberam resignacionem Ricd. Marshall. Lib. Instit.]		

In testo' Rob. Hoo nup. de Blyburgh 1503. I give to ye welfare of the Church of Thorington 3 acres of Land ther lyyng by the town land. Rix. 24.

End of the entries in Tanner's MS.

Books of Institution.	Dates.	Rectors.	Patrons.
Lib. xiii. 52.	{ 27 April, 1505.	Eliseus Aynesworth,	....
Lib. xiv. 31.	per mortem Rob'ti Smyth.		
„ „ 89.	{ 3 Aug. 1509.	Thomas Benewike,	....
	per mortem Elesei Ailmer.		
Lib. xv. 155.	{ 3 Aug. 1509.	Thomas Bonwyk,	....
	per mortem Elisei Ailm.		
„ „ 75.	5 Aug. 1514.	Robertus Dracots, LL.B.	{ Episcopus per lapsum. (Collated by lapse.)
Lib. xvi. 61.	7 Maij, 1521.	Willimus Pankill.*	Prior et conventus de Blyburgh.

per liberam resignacionem Robti. Draycotts, *on an annual pension of 20ˢ settled by the Vicar General.*

P'stit iuramet' (Prestitit Juramentum) de p'solvendo p'dicto mag'ro Robert Draycotts Resignanti annua' pensione' viginti solidoru' de fructibus et prouentibus (*prouentus, produce*) dicte eccl'ie iuxta modu' et forma' limitac'onis ordinac'onis & assignac'onis dicti vicarii generalis in eâ parte l'time (*legitime*) fact'.

The only mention of retirement on pension.

| Lib. xvii. 52. | } 27 Maii, 1554. | Johannes Hanson, A.M., | Ricardus Freston, miles. |
| „ „ 63. | per mortem ultimi Rectoris. | | |

The first mention of a Lay Patron.

| „ „ 214. | 26 Jan. 1558. | Antonius Wilkensonne. | Episcopus per lapsum. |

per liberam resignationem m'ri Johannis Hanson in artibus m'ri ultimi ac nuper Rectoris sine Incumbentis ib'm vacan' Et ad suam collationem per lapsum semestris temporis jure sibi l'time devoluto hâc vice spectan' Dilecto sibi in X'po Domino Anthonio Wilkensonne vicario de Brampfilde intuitu charitatis contulit Ipsu'q' Rectorem in eadem canonice instituit cum suis juribus et pertinenciis universq' Et dicta eccl'ia de Thorington prefate vicarie de Brampfilde propter ipsius exhibitatem tenuitatem et paupertatem ac propter certas alias causas unita et annexa fuit pro tempore Incumbentis etc. . . .

This is the first mention of pluralities of Livings.

| Lib. xix. 174. | 9 Jan. 1571. | Thomas Moins. | Episcopus per lapsum. |

(*Thomas Mons, Parson, was buried at Thorington,* 17 *June,* 1573.)

---

* "Will'us Payngell, Rector de Thorington, testis cartæ dat. 36 H. VIII. Thorington Deeds, 19." Note in Davy's MSS. Thorington, fol. 400.—T. S. H.

Books of Institution.	Dates.	Rectors.	Patrons.
Lib. xix. 195.	14 Aug. 1573.	Johannes Denney.	Arthur Hopton Edmund Hall arm. et Willim. Roberdsgen.

per mortem Thome Moynes ...... ad presentac'o'em discretor' virorum Arthuri Hopton Edmundi Halle Armigeroru' et Willimi Roberds generosi ratione Dimissionis ad firmu' manerii de Blyburghe pro termino annor' nondum finitorum veroru' ipsius eccl'ie patronoru' hac vice spectan' ......

| „ „ 222. | 1 Oct. 1593. | Robertus Goold, A.M. | Edwardus Coke, ar. |

per liberam resignacionem Johannis Denny. Ad presentac'o'em egregij viri Edwardi Coke ar. Solicitat d'ue Regine hac vice tantu' spectan' Subscriptis prius per eum articulis suscepte Religionis in hoc Regno Anglie iuxta forma' Statuti &c. ac etiam prestito iuramento de refutand' et renu'ciand' omni et o'imod' iurisdictioni aucti' et superioritati foraneis et extraneis, ac de agnoscendo suprema' auct'em Regiam in hoc Regno Anglie &c. necnon de canonica ob'ia (obedientia) etc.

First mention of the oaths submitting to Royal supremacy.

| Lib. xxii. 28. | 2 Oct. 1610. | Samuel Ledys, A.M. | Sir Ed. Coke, Knt. |

per cessionem ultimi Rectoris.

[*Lib. xxii. 24. 21 Nov. 1609, Robert Gould, A.M., was instituted to the Rectory of Tittleshall, vacant by the death of the last Incumbent, on the presentation of Sir Ed. Coke, Knt.*]

| „ „ 36 | 16 April, 1612. | Robertus Gould, A.M. | Sir Ed. Coke, Knt. |

per resignationem ultimi Rectoris.

[*Robert Gould was buried in Thorington Church, 13 July, 1620. M.I.*]

" *Francis Kynnaston, Rector Ecclesiæ de Thorington,*" *signs the baptismal register in* 1620. *His institution to the Rectory is not recorded in the Institution Books. At that time, for four or five years, the Books of Institution were not accurately kept, Bishop Jegon dying in* 1617, *and his successor, Bishop Overall, in* 1619. *He was summoned to attend the Bishop's Visitation in* 1627, *but did not do so. Francis Kynaston matriculated at Oriel*

Books of Institution.	Dates.	Rectors.	Patrons.

College, Oxford, 11 Dec. 1601, *aged* 14 ; *he was eldest son of a Knight, co. Salop.*

Lib. xxiv. 19.　27 Oct. 1610.　　Johannes Peirson, A.M.　　Henry Coke,
per resignationem Francisci Kenaston.　　　　　　　　　Esq.

A Dispensation was granted him to hold Bramfield with Thorington.

[On the inside of the cover of the first Register Book is this memorandum made by " S. M. Westhorp, Curate of Thorington, March 18th *1843." N.B.—John Peirson was afterwards Bishop of Chester, Author of work on the Creeds, etc. This, however, is an error, as John Peirson was dead in* 1646, *and the name is spelt differently. John Pearson, D.D., was instituted to Terrington St. Clement, co. Norfolk, in* 1660, *and in the Index of Institutions to parishes held in " Union," referring to John Peirson's dispensation to hold Thorington with Bramfield, Terrington has been erroneously written instead of Thorington. This accounts for the mistake made by Mr. Kitson, Bishop's Registrar of Norwich, who sent the above statement to Mr. Westhorp.]*

„　„ 58.　31 March, 1646.　Johannes Chunne, A.M.　　Henry Coke,
per mortem Johannis Peirson.　　　　　　　　　　　　　Esq.

John Chunne, Clerk, was buried 22 July, 1659.

Lib. xxv. 25.　22 Oct. 1661.　　Willimus Evans, A.M.　　Henry Coke,
per mortem Johannis Chunne.　　　　　　　　　　　　Esq.

A dispensation was on the same day granted him to hold Bramfield with Thorington.

Lib. xxvii. 3.　25 Nov. 1676.　Johannes Mayhew, A.M.　　Robert
per mortem [blank] Evans.　　　　　　　　　　　　　Coke, Esq.

He was of Catharine Hall, Cambridge, A.B. 1662 ; *A.M.* 1666. *In Lib.* xxviii. 32, 24 *Feb.* 1687, *a dispensation was granted to him to hold the Rectory of Holton with Thorington, to which he was then presented by K. James II., Patron. John Mayhew was buried* 28 *Sep.* 1693, *in Thorington Churchyard. M.I. His headstone is the oldest memorial stone there.*

Lib. xxviii. 128.　10 July, 1694.　　Thomas Shortrudge.　　John Bence.
per mortem ultimi Rectoris.　　　　　　　　　　　　　Esq.

He matriculated at Exeter College, Oxford, 18 *July,* 1679, *aged* 16, *son of the Rev. Hugh Shortrudge of Ashreyny, co. Devon; B.A. St.*

Books of Institution.	Dates.	Rectors.	Patrons.
	Alban Hall, 1683. On the same day that he was instituted to Thorington a dispensation was granted to him to hold Thorington with Hallisworth, to which he had been instituted [p. 67] 16 *April*, 1690, "*per Dianam Baronissam de Wymonley curatricem Egidii Baronis de Wymonley (durante minoritate suâ).*" *Buried at Halesworth 22 July*, 1722.		
Lib. xxix. 207.	7 Aug. 1722.	Thomas Bence, A.M. By the death of Thomas Shortrudge. *He was of Catharine Hall, Cambridge; A.B.* 1699; *A.M.* 1703. On the same day a dispensation was granted to him to hold Thorington with Kelsale-cum-Carlton, to which he had been instituted [*Lib.* xxviii. 201] 23 *April,* 1705, *on the presentation of John Bence, Esq. Buried at Carlton 27 Sep.* 1757, *aged 78-9.* M. I.	Alexander Bence, Esq.
Lib. xxx. 168.	13 Dec. 1753.	Charles Mabourn, A.B. On the resignation of Thomas Bence. *He was of Caius College, Cambridge; A.B.* 1733. On the same day a dispensation was granted him to hold Thorington with the Vicarage of Bramfield, to which he had been instituted [p. 91] 20 *Dec.* 1737. *K. Geo. II., Patron. Buried at Bramfield 20 Jan.* 1758.*	Alexander Bence, Esq.
Lib. xxx. 195.	6 Feb. 1758.	Barnabas Symonds, A.B. By the death of Charles Mabourn. *He was of Caius College, Cambridge; A.B.* 1745. *Buried at Kelsale* 20 *June*, 1782.†	Alexander Bence, Esq.

* The following notice of Charles Mabourn is taken from Davy's MSS., Thorington, fol. 400. "In the name of God, Amen. I Charles Mabourn of Bramfield, co. Suffolk, Clerk, etc. "First, I do hereby make ..... Hannah Copping of Bramfield, af'sd, Sp', to be sole executrix of this my will, and do direct that she shall pay all my just debts .... as soon after my decease as conveniently may be, and after the same shall be fully paid .... then I give .... all the rest .... unto the said Hannah Copping her Ex'tors .... and I do hereby make void all former wills by me made. Dated 5 Oct. 1737. Proved 9 Feb. 1758 at Norwich. "From the Probate in possession of Rev. Geo. Turner, 1856. "Mr. Mabourn was Rector of Thorington, and was to have been married to the abovementioned Hannah Copping, who, after his death, married John Talbot of Brampton, gent."

† In Davy's MSS., Thorington, fol. 400, are the following notices of Barnabas Symonds:— "He was Rector of Thorington, and Master of the School at Kelsale, where he constantly resided. He was author of a 'Treatise on Field Diversions,' of which a second edition was published in 1823.

He was patronised by the Blois family, and was sent to Cambridge by a subscription among his friends. He was possessed of a considerable degree of humour, which appeared in several instances while he was at Cambridge. The following was told me (Aug. 1823) by Rev. Wm.

C

Books of Institution.	Dates.	Rectors.	Patrons.
Lib. xxxi. 173.	23 Dec. 1782.	George Golding Graves, M.A. By death of Barnabas Symonds.	George Golding, Esq., and Anne his wife.

He matriculated from Univ. Coll. Oxon, 1774, aged 18, son of William Graves, Gent., of Westminster; B.A. 1778; M.A. 1781. A dispensation was granted him (he had then assumed the name of Golding) 9 February, 1787 [p. 208], to hold Thorington with Kelsale-cum-Carlton. Patrons: G. Golding, Esq., and Ann his wife. Buried at St. Margaret's, Westminster, 10 March, 1806. The Act of Parliament legalising his change of name was passed in 1804.

Lib. xxxii. 113.	23 Oct. 1806.	Bence Bence, LL.B. By death of George Golding Golding.	Himself.

Browne of Marlesford, who was his nephew:—A large party was expected to dine with the Master of Caius College one day, and as was usual, the preparations for the purpose were made early in the day. Symonds contrived to get unobserved into the Hall, and collecting all the forks laid for the guests, stuck them in and about the carving over the Master's chair representing the arms of the College. This was not observed till the dinner was served, and when the guests found that no forks were provided for them, the Master took the butler severely to task for his neglect, and threatened to discharge him from his situation; and he could not be pacified till some one observed how they had been employed, when the joke produced a general laugh, and luckily the author escaped for that time undiscovered, and of course avoided punishment, though the butler afterwards found out who it was who was so nearly the cause of his dismission.

On another occasion he had a still narrower escape from a severe castigation. The Dean of the College, whose duty it was to read prayers in Chapel, had a very peculiar mode of reading, and that a very disagreeable one. One afternoon Symonds, who sat nearly under him, and who was a good mimic, made the responses in a tone and manner so exactly resembling the Dean as to produce more than a smile among all the auditors. This was an offence too flagrant to be overlooked; he was accordingly convened before the Master, who severely reprimanded him for the impropriety and indecency of his conduct, and declared his intention of inflicting a very severe punishment upon him. Symonds, with all due respect, requested to be heard in his defence, and having received permission, stated that he had been sent to college by a subscription of his friends, with the intention that he should qualify himself for Orders, that he had come to the College with the determination of paying every attention to what he should hear and see, and to guide himself accordingly, that though the mode in which the Dean read the service in Chapel was certainly different from what he had been accustomed to hear, yet that he thought that he was bound to consider it the proper mode, and had endeavoured to the best of his power to imitate it, and that if he had judged wrong, he had not erred intentionally, and was very sorry for it; that this was the sole motive for his conduct, and he should be very sorry if he had offended the Dean, or had been guilty of any impropriety towards the College. This was all said with so much apparent earnestness and simplicity as to remove the Master's anger, who dismissed him with a caution that he did not in future subject himself to a similar reprehension,

The son of Barnabas Symonds, who was brought up to the study of physic, and practised for many years as a surgeon and apothecary at Saxmundham, had all the humour of his father, and all his love for practical jokes. Many are the stories told of him in his neighbourhood, and many the pranks still remembered about him. He has declined practice, but still (1826) resides in the same town."

Books of Institution.	Dates.	Rectors.	Patrons.

He was of Emmanuel College, Cambridge; LL.B. 1771. He had been instituted [Lib. xxxi. 95] 5 Nov. 1774, as Bence Sparrow, to the Rectory of Beccles, on the resignation of Peter Routh, the father of the Rev. Martin Joseph Routh, D.D., the celebrated President of Magdalen College, Oxford, on the presentation of Ann Sparrow of Beccles, widow, and Mary Bence of Henstead, spinster; and 1 April, 1786 [Lib. xxxi. 197], to the Rectory of Kettleburgh, himself being Patron for this turn. He resigned both these Rectories, 1806, and on 23 Oct. 1806, he was instituted (having assumed the name of Bence in 1804) to the Rectories of Thorington and Kelsale-cum-Carlton, on his own presentation; on the next day, 24 Oct. 1806, he was reinstituted to Beccles, and 20 April, 1814 [Lib. xxxii. 184], he was licensed to the Perpetual Curacy of Redisham Magna, on the presentation of Robert Sparrow of Worlingham Hall, Esq. He resigned Kelsale-cum-Carlton 1810, and Thorington, 1821. Buried at Beccles, 17 Sept. 1824. M.I.

Lib. xxxiii. 18.   27 Sep. 1821.   Lancelot Robert Browne, A.B.   Rev. Bence
                    By resignation of Bence Bence.   Bence.
He was of St. John's College, Cambridge; A.B. 1808; A.M. 1819. On the same day a dispensation was granted to him to hold Thorington with Kelsale-cum-Carlton, to which he had been instituted 9 July, 1810 [Lib. xxxii. 141], on resignation of Bence Bence, and on his presentation; and on 27 Dec. 1826 [Lib. xxxiii. 79], a dispensation was granted him to hold Saxmundham also, vacant by the death of William Brown. Patron: Dudley Long North, Esq., of Little Glemham Hall. Died 11 Feb. 1868, and buried at Kelsale.* M.I.

* The following notice of his family occurs in the 'Gentleman's Magazine,' Jan. 1830, p. 89 :—
"Died Dec. 20, 1829, at Conington in Cambridgeshire, aged 68, the Rev. Thomas Brown, Rector of that parish for more than forty years, and a Magistrate for the counties of Cambridge and Hunts. Mr. Brown was third and youngest son of Lancelot Brown, Esq., Head Gardener to his late Majesty at Hampton Court, who was celebrated in the last century (under the better known appellation of Capability Brown) for his skill in laying out parks and ornamental gardening, by which he acquired a large estate of his own, which passed to the subject of this memoir, after his two elder brothers had enjoyed it in succession, and had died without issue, viz., Lancelot, a Barrister, and sometime M.P. for Huntingdon ; and John, an Admiral of the Royal Navy. [On the 9th inst., died at Bath the Rev. George Brown, late of Puckle-

Books of Institution.	Dates.	Rectors.	Patrons.
Lib. xxxiv. 76.	15 Dec. 1849.	Thomas Starkie Bence, A.M. By cession of Lancelot Robert Brown. *He was of St. John's College, Cambridge; A.B. 1848; A.M. 1851. Buried at Thorington 20 July, 1858. Memorial window.*	Henry Bence Bence, Esq.
„ „ 171.	18 Nov. 1858.	Addison Bramwell, A.B. By death of Thomas Starkie Bence. *He was of Trinity College, Cambridge; A.B. 1854.*	Henry Bence Bence, Esq.
Lib. xxxv. 30.	24 Oct. 1871.	William Belcher, A.B. By resignation of Addison Bramwell. *He was of Trinity College, Dublin.*	{ Henry Alexander Starkie Bence, Esq.
„ „ 90.	16 June, 1876.	Thomas Smyth Hill, B.C.L., M.A. By cession of William Belcher, now Rector of Heveningham, co. Suffolk. *He was of Magdalen College, Oxford; B.C.L. 1819; M.A. 1865.*	H. A. S. Bence, Esq.

church, Gloucestershire, and of Sydney College, Cambridge, son of the late Lancelot Brown, Esq., M.P. for Huntingdon.—'Ipswich Journal,' July 24, 1819.] The late Mr. Brown was of St. John's College, Cambridge; B.A. 1784; M.A. 1787; and was presented to the Rectory of Conington in 1789, by the Hon. Dr. Yorke, then Bishop of Ely. He married, early in life, Susan, daughter of Dr. Dickins, Rector of Hemingford Gray, near Huntingdon, and by her, who survives him [*she died at Saxmundham 18 Jan. 1833, in the seventy-third year of her age*]. he has left two sons. Lancelot, Rector of Kelsale in Suffolk, who succeeds to his estate; and Thomas Charles, Curate of Somersham, in the Isle of Ely, a living attached to the Regius Professorship of Divinity in the University of Cambridge; and one daughter, Susan. The remains of Mr. Brown were deposited by those of his father under the monument in the chancel of Fenstanton."

MEMORANDUM OF COKE,

AND

GIFT OF THE CHURCH BELL.

On the second page of the First Book of Registers is the following Memorandum:—

"MEMORANDU' y^t ye Right worshipfull Edward Coke Esquier Attourny Generall to the Queenes most excellent maiestie and Bridgett his wife did Giue unto the Towneshippe of Thorington in June 1598 one Bell* alone vppon this condicion that neyther the Churchwardens nor any of the inhabitants of the said Towne should at any time after ye aforesaid Guift sell awaye the said Bell but continve and maintayne the same for the callinge together of the inhabitants of the said Towne to divine Service and other Seemely vses In witnes whereof I Robert Golde minister of the saide Towne of Thorington have sett to my hand to this wrightinge the xxth of September 1607.

ROBERT' GOLDE."

In the 'Life of Sir Edward Coke,'† by Cuthbert William Johnson, are the following notices:—

Edward Coke was the only son of Robert Coke of Mileham, co. Norfolk, Bencher of Lincoln's Inn, and Winifred, daughter and coheiress of William Knightley of Morgrave Knightley, in the same county. He was born Feb. 1, and baptized Feb. 8, 1551, at Mileham; matriculated Trin. Coll. Camb. Oct. 25, 1567; entered at Clifford's Inn, London, 1571, and at the Inner Temple, 1572; married, Aug. 13, 1582, at Cookeley, Bridget, daughter and coheiress of John Paston, Esq., of Huntingfield Hall, co. Suffolk, by whom he had seven sons and three daughters.

1585. Recorder of Coventry.
1587. Recorder of Norwich.
1590. Bencher of the Inner Temple, and Steward of the Manor of Framlingham.
1592. Recorder of London; Reader of the Inner Temple; Solicitor General, and M.P. for Norfolk.
1593. Speaker of the House of Commons, and Attorney General.
1598. His wife died (according to the inscription on her monument in Tittleshall Church) June 27, and the Register records her burial July 24.

---

* Round the crown of the bell is this inscription:—
    Danwell Owen made me for Waneted, 1596, with a ma-onic triangle.
In the Terriers the bell is described as weighing about one hundred weight.
† London: Henry Colburn. 1837.

Before he had been many months a widower he married, 2ndly, Lady Elizabeth, 4th daughter of Thomas Cecil, first Earl of Exeter, the beautiful, young, and wealthy widow of Sir William Hatton. "The marriage ceremony was performed in a private house, without either banns or licence. In consequence of this irregularity, Coke and his lady, with the Rev. Henry Bathwell, Rector of Okeover, Thomas Lord Burleigh, afterwards Earl of Exeter, the bride's father, and several others present at the marriage, were prosecuted in the Archbishop's Court. By a timely and respectful submission, however, by their proxies, they escaped the greater excommunication."

1603. Knighted by James I.
1606. King's Sergeant, and Lord Chief Justice of the Common Pleas.
1613. Chief Justice of the Court of King's Bench, usually called Chief Justice of England, and Privy Councillor.
1614. High Steward of the University of Cambridge.
1616. "Removed" from the Court of King's Bench. Described by Sir George Croke as "a prudent, grave, and learned man in the common laws of the realm, and of a pious and virtuous life."
1617. M.P. for Norfolk.
1620. M.P. for Liskeard.
1623. M.P. for Coventry, after having been committed to the Tower as one of the "illtempered spirits" that opposed the Court.
1625. High Sheriff of Bucks. M.P. for Norfolk.
1627. M.P. for Bucks.
1632. "The third of May, riding in the morning in Stoke, between eight and nine o'clock, to take the ayre, my horse under me had a strange stumble backwards, and fell upon me (being above eighty years old), where my head lighted near to sharp stubbes, and the heavy horse upon me. And yet, by the providence of Almighty God, though I was in the greatest danger, yet I had not the least hurt—nay, no hurt at all."
1633. [*Misprint for* 1634.] Died Sep. 3. His last words being, "Thy kingdom come, Thy will be done." While on his death-bed, Sir Francis Windebank came to his house at Stoke in virtue of an order from the Privy Council in search of certain seditious papers—at least this was the pretence. He carried away Coke's will, and several other papers and manuscripts. Seven years afterwards the papers were principally returned, but not the will.
1634. Buried Oct. 4, in Tittleshall Church, co. Norfolk. For his monument £400 was paid to Nicholas Stone.

"So devout a son he was of the Church of England, in the observance of the rites and ceremonies thereof, that I am confident that in near forty years before his death, if sickness or public employment, or something extraordinary did not divert him, scarce one day passed wherein he was not twice a devout assistant in the offering up of the public service of the Church; nor was he less severe to himself in his person, than just to his public employments, being never so much as suspected of any notorious or scandalous vice. ('Justice Vindicated.' Roger Coke. 1660.)

REGISTERS OF THORINGTON.

Before the suppression of Monasteries by Hen. VIII., Registers of marriages and burials of persons connected with them were kept by each house, also of those who were baptized or buried within their precincts. In 1538 an order was issued that each parish should keep a Register of christenings, marriages, and burials, but this order was not generally obeyed, and in 1597 another order was issued by the Convocation of Canterbury, and confirmed by the Queen, that such Registers should be kept, and that copies of such Registers as had been hitherto made, should be made in the new books, and each page attested by the signatures of the Incumbent and Churchwardens. In this parish of Thorington the Register seems to have been commenced in 1561, and copies from y̆ ould booke, which does not now exist, made in 1593, down to the marriage of James Crispe and Abra' Brooke, June 17, and each page is attested by the signatures of Robert' Golde, Rector, and Will'm Spalding and Thoms Johnsonn, Churchwardens.

It will be observed that in the earlier portions of the Registers surnames are sometimes spelt in different ways, and that the dates are occasionally intermixed. The Rectors of Thorington seem to have adopted the plan in general use among the Clergy of keeping a book for entries to be made by the clerk, and copying these entries when they had to present their Registers at the Visitations.

It should be remembered that before 1752 the year commenced on March 25, and not on Jan. 1.

ANNO DOMINI 1561.

Christnings.	Dec. 31.	Roberte Dawsone was borne, beinge a basterde.
	Jan. 5.	Elizabeth Reade was borne.
	Feb. 28.	George Seppence was borne.
Mariages.	Oct. 1.	Henry Burter and Maryan Daye, widdowe.
	June 1.	Robert Drwery and Elizabeth Daye.
	Oct. 10.	Bartlemwe Baldry and Tomasine Smyth.
	Oct. 15.	William Pynner and Margret Momforde.
Burialls.	Ap. 26.	Henry Daye.
	July 2.	Katharine Daye.
	July 10.	Francis Crispe.

ANNO DOMINI 1562.

Christenings.	Sep. 6.	George Hill was borne.
	Jan. 10.	Robert Ffarrare was borne.
	Feb. 20.	Richarde Burter was borne.
Burialls.	Feb. 1.	Roberte farrare.
	March 1.	Richard Burter.

ANNO DOMINI 1563.

Christnings.	March 31.	George Rooke was borne.
	June 27.	Anne Cutberde was borne.

	Aug. 15.	Bridget Marks was borne.
	Oct. 4.	George Russell was borne.
	March 10.	Anne Reade was borne.
Mariags.	Feb. 20.	Thomas Marchant and Alice Dowsine, widdowe.
Buryalls.	March 6.	Katharine Burture.
	Dec. 28.	Katharine Marchant.

ANNO DOMINI 1564.

Christenings.	Sep. 10.	George Pynner was borne.
	Oct. 5.	Chaleb Richard was borne.
	Jan. 2.	Elizabeth Covell was borne.
	Feb. 20.	Christopher Russell was borne.
Mariags.	July 3.	John Merser and Anne Meene, widdowe.

ANNO DOM. 1565.

Christenings.	March 26.	John farrare was borne.
	Ap. 24.	Elizabeth Cutberde was borne.
	Maye 3.	ffrancis Seppens was borne.
	Jan. 31.	Alice Smith was borne.

ANNO DOM. 1566.

Christenings.	July 26.	ffreseworth Hedde daughter of Robert Hedde and Anne his wife.
	Oct. 24.	John Pynner sonne of William Pynner and Anne his wife.
	Dec. 22.	George Paine sonne of John Payne and Mande his wife.
Mariags.	May 3.	Robert Hedde and Anne Gardler.
	May 12.	Robert fosdicke and Ellyne Porter.
Burialls.	July 7.	Anne ffarrare.
	Dec. 20.	Trystram Lamle.
	Dec. 28.	Anne Payne.
	Dec. 31.	Susane Seppens.

ANNO DOM. 1567.

Christenings.	Feb. 7.	John Moulton sonne of Edmonde and Julyan his wife.
	March 24.	Elizabeth Hedde daughter of Robert Hedde and Anne his wife.
	May 5.	Thomas Grene sonne of Roger Grene and Margret his wife.
Mariags.	Dec. 1.	John Persse and Margret Hutton.

ANNO DOMINI 1568.

Christenings.	March 23.	Mary Pynner daughter of William Pynner and Margrette his wife.
	Dec. 27.	Robert Marchant sonne of Bartlemewe and Joane his wife.
Mariags.	Oct. 31.	Robert Porpose and Mary Smyth.

ANNO DOM. 1569.

Christninges.	May 27.	Em'e Moulton daughter of Edmond Moulton and Julyan his wife
	July 31.	George Porpose sonne of Robert Porpose and Mary his wife
Burialls.	June 24.	Jhone Dobbes

1570. deest.
1571. deest.
1572. deest.

ANNO DOM. 1573.

Christenings.	Aug. 16.	Reynolde Moulton sonne unto Edmonde Moulton and Julian his wife
	Aug. 24.	Martha Ingram daughter to Thomas Ingram and Marrible his wife
	Nov. 15.	Henry Som'ers sonne to Robert Sommers and Annys his wife
	Nov. 22.	Allice Porte daughter to Thomas Porte and Elizabeth his wife
Mariags.	Feb. 6.	Reynold Reve and Margret Sepens
Burialls.	May 5.	Ham'ond Russell sonne of John Russell
	June 17.	Thomas Mons. Parson [See Institutions, 1571.]
	June 22.	Henry Deye
	Jan. 28.	Henry Som'ers sonne unto Robert Sommers

ANNO DOM. 1574.

Christenings.	Jan 2.	John Reve sonne unto Reynolde Reve
	Jan. 30.	Thomas Som'ers sonne unto Robert Som'ers
Mariags.	Dec. 30.	John Gylny and Margret Bucknam
Burialls.	Feb. 17.	Joane Donnet wife of Roberte Donnet

ANNO DOM. 1575.

Christenings.	June 12.	Bridget Moulton daughter unto Edmond Moulton and Julian his wife
	Jan. 19.	Margret Porte daughter unto Thomas Porte and Elizabeth his wife
Mariags.	May 8.	Robert Dowtie and Jane Houlseby
	May 15.	Henry Crispe and Alice ffevareycare
	July 4.	Robert Donnet and Joane Coreye
Burialls.		None

ANNO DOM. 1576.

Christenings.	June 24.	Em'e Donnet daughter unto Roberte Donnet and Joane his wife
	Sep. 26.	Julyan Thurston daughter unto Thomas Thurston and Margret his wife

D

ANNO DOM. 1577.

Christenings.	May 16.	Bridget Wells daughter unto William Welles and Margery his wife
	June 29.	John Crispe sonne unto Henrye Crispe and Alice his wife
	Oct. 6.	Dorothie fellowe daughter unto Edward fellowe and Christiane his wife [wife
	Oct. 27.	William Donnet sonne of Robert Donnet and Joane his
	Feb. 16.	Jane Burges daughter unto John Burges and Christian his wife
Mariags.	Jan. 21.	James Meyes and Elizabeth Baroe
Burialls.	Oct. 2.	John Crispe sonne of Henry Crispe and Alice his wife
	Nov. 4.	Dorothie fellowe daughter of Edward fellowe and Christian his wife
	Feb. 16.	Dorothee Russell wife of John Russell

ANNO DOM. 1578.

Christenings.	Sep. 14.	William Porte sonne unto Thomas Porte and Elizabeth his wife
	Oct. 5.	Edmond Moulton sonne unto Edmond Moulton and Julyan his wife
	Oct. 12.	Chatherine Crispe daughter unto Henry Crispe and Alice his wife
	March 8.	John Woodcocke sonne unto William Woodecocke and Elizabeth his wife
Burialls.	Sep. 24.	Thomas Porte [his wife
	Nov. 15.	Allice Porte daughter unto Thomas Porte and Elizabeth

ANNO DOM. 1579.

Christenings.	Sep. 20.	Roberte Donnet sonne unto Robert Donnet and Joane his wife
	Dec. 9.	Em'e fellowe daughter unto Edward fellowe and Christian his wife

ANNO DOM. 1580.

Christenings.	Sep. 25.	Henry Thurston sonne unto Thomas Thurston and Margret his wife [his wife
	March 19.	Robert Dowtie sonne unto Robert Dowtie and Jane
Mariags.	Sep. 22.	William Barbare and Elizabeth Porte widdowe
Burials.	July 30.	Anne Reve wife unto Robert Reve

ANNO DOM. 1581.

Christenings.	July 20.	Nicholas Reve sonne unto Roberte Reve and Anne his wife : which cannot be trwe for his mother died the yeare before, there is mention made in the ould booke of this Nicholas birth the 19th of Julye but no yeare of our Lorde sett downe : onelye it is sett after ye yeare 1578

	May 2.	Philippe Woodecocke sonne unto William Woodcocke and Elizabeth his wife
	July 30.	Annys Wells daughter unto William Welles and Margery his wife
	Aug. 15.	Robert Moulton sonne unto Edmond Moulton and Julyan his wife
	Sep. 24.	Mathewe Denny sonne unto John Denny and Joane his wife
	Oct. 15.	Mary Crispe daughter unto Henry Crispe and Allice his wife
Mariages.	Feb. 6.	Hammo'd Seppens and Joane fellowe widdowe
Burialls.	May 6.	John Houlseby
	Jan. 26.	Mary Coxe wife of Thomas Coxe

ANNO DOM. 1582.

Christenings.	May 1.	Nicholas Everard sonne unto Nicholas Everard and Margret his wife
	Oct. 28.	Henry Donnet sonne unto Robert Donnet and Joane his wife
Mariags.	Sep. 17.	Anthonie Donnet and Elizabeth Seppens
	Oct. 10.	Thomas Coxe and Jane Woodwarde
Burialls.	Sep. 14.	William Seppens

ANNO DOM. 1583.

Christenings.	Aug. 11.	Nicholas Thurston sonne unto Thomas Thurston and Margret his wife
	Sep. 1.	Robert Thurston sonne unto John Thurston
	Sep. 18.	Mary Moulton daughter unto Edmond Moulton and Julyan his wife
	Sep. 24.	Isaach Woodcocke sonne unto William Woodcocke and Elizabeth his wife
Mariags.	April 18.	Robert french of Carleton Covill widower and Anne Stamforde
	Oct. 7.	Amos Clarke and Mary Feveryear
	Nov. 18.	Henry Marcon of Westleton widdower and Allice Corey of Silam singlewoman
Burialls.	Sep. 5.	Anne Thurston daughter unto John Thurston

ANNO DOMINI 1584.

Christenings.	April 26.	Margery Denny daughter unto John Denny and Joane his wife
	May 1.	Williame Evered sonne unto Nicholas Evered and Margret his wife
	Sep. 4.	John Weste and Juliane Weste sonne and daughter unto John West and Rose his wife
	Oct. 25.	Bridget Donnet daughter unto Anthony Donnet and Elizabeth his wife

Mariags.	Jan. 13.	Roberte Coke servant to Mr Dunne of Blyborough and Anne Browne
	Sep. 6.	William Wake and Mary Clarke
Burialls.	Aug. 16.	Robert Donnet servant unto William Woodcocke

ANNO DOM. 1585.

Christenings.	Feb. 22.	Joane Donnet daughter unto Robert Donnet and Joane his wife
	March 14.	Mary Clarke daughter to Amos Clark and Mary his wife
	April 12.	John Evered sonne unto Nicholas Evered and Margret his wife
	May 16.	William Wiseman sonne unto John Wiseman and Mary his wife
	Sep. 2.	Alice Thurston daughter unto Thomas Thurston and Margret his wife
	Sep. 26.	Robert fellowe sonne unto Edward fellowe and Christian his wife
	Jan. 23.	Thomas Aytone sonne unto Stephen Ayeton and Annys his wife
	Feb. 2.	John Wiseman sonne to John Wiseman aud Mary his wife was baptized the second of february 1585. this John was left ont of ye ould booke
Mariags.	Feb. 3.	William fenninge and Annys Grene
Burialls.	Jan. 22.	Margret foxe
	Aug. 12.	William Wiseman sonne unto John Wisema' and Mary his wife
	Oct. 16.	William Evered sonne unto Nicholas

ANNO DOM. 1586.

Christenings.	May 15.	Elizabeth Moulton daughter unto Edmond Moulton and Julyan his wife
	Jan. 15.	Emme Weste daughter unto John West and Rose his [wife
Mariages.	Oct. 10.	Richard foxe and Katharine feveryeare
Burialls.	July 22.	Elizabeth Ayeton daughter unto Stephen Ayeton and Annys his wife

ANNO DOM. 1587.

Christenings.	Sep. 17.	Henry Clarke sonne unto Amos Clarke and Mary his wife
	Oct. 1.	Henry Evered sonne unto Nicholas Evered and Margret his wife
Mariags.	Jan. 18.	Robert Deaves and Elizabeth Arnold

ANNO DOM. 1588.

Christenings.	May 27.	Thomas foxe sonne to Richarde foxe and Katharine his wife
Mariages.	Sep. 22.	William Carman and Katharine Manninge

ANNO DOM. 1589.

Christnings.	June 1.	Jasone fellowe daughter unto Edwarde fellowe and Christian his wife
	Oct. 26.	Thomas Carman soune unto William Carman and Katharine his wife [wife
	Nov. 16.	Elizabeth West daughter unto John Weast and Rose his
Mariages.	Aug. 28.	Arthure Ellys and Margret Rushe of Darsham
	Oct. 13.	Henry Girlinge and Elizabeth Mannwell
Burialls.	April 20.	Nicholas Evered
	June 2.	Edwarde fellowe

ANNO DOM. 1590.

Christenings.	Sep. 27.	Mathewe Wiseman sonne to John Wiseman and Mary his wife
Mariages.	April 23.	John Houldage of Woodbridge and Sisly Morfill
	Dec. 14.	William Morrell and Rabecca feveryeare
Burialls.	Aug. 7.	Jason fellowe daughter unto Edwarde fellowe and Christian his wife
	Feb. 1.	Alice Houlseby widowe

ANNO DOM. 1591.

Christenings.	April 5.	John Thurston sonne unto Thomas Thurston and Margret his wife [his wife
	April 25.	Henry Bearte sonne unto Roberte Bearte and Annys
Mariages.	June 29.	John Rackam and Joane Grenewoode
Burialls.	Dec. 8.	It. one Derrowe a ladde of the age of viiith yeares whoe as he saide came from Bunggay and was there borne he dyed at our bricke Kell and was buried the viiith of December*

ANNO DOM. 1592.

Mariages.	May 21.	Thomas Seppens and Avis Buttyvannte
	Sep. 25.	Symon Betts and Margret Smyth [his wife
Burials.	May 26.	Alice Clareke daughter unto Amos Clareke and Mary

ANNO DOM. 1593.

Christenings.	March 17.	Margret Crispe daughter to James Crispe and Abra his wife. R. R. G.†
Mariages.	May 18.	Roger Berry and Margery Denny by licence from Norw^{ch}
	June 17.	James Crispe and Abra Brooke

---

* *The brick kiln has long disappeared, but "Kiln-meadow," "Great" and "Little Kiln-fields," and a plantation called "Earth-holes" adjoining the keeper's house in the Park, probably indicate the site of the "bricke Kell."*

† *I can give no explanation of these initials, which seem to be in Robert Golde's handwriting, unless it be that they indicate the termination of the entries in the old book, and the two marriages that follow are added as belonging to the old registers, having taken place between the resignation of John Denney and his own institution.*

Baptismes Robertus Golde Rector Ecclesiæ de Thoxington. Anno Dom: 1593.

(*Robert Golde here begins the registers of his own incumbency, and heads the page as above.*)

1594.	April 28.	Thomas Clarke sonne to Amos Clark and Mary his wife
	Nov. 24.	Robert Emans sonne to George Emans and Dyonys his wife
	March 22.	John Gurny sonne to John Gurny
1595.		nulla
1596.		nulla
1597.	Aug. 7.	Anne Johnsone daughter to Thomas Johnsone and Elizabeth his wife
	Feb. 26.	Margery Wiseman daughter to John Wiseman and Elizabeth his wife
1598.	April 25.	ffrancys Seppens sonne to francys Seppens and Margret his wife
	May 28.	William Emans sonne of George Emans and Dyonys his wife
	March 22.	Thomas Johnsone sonne to Thomas Johnsone and Elizabeth his wife
1599.	Nov. 22.	Rose Lewes daughter to John Lewes and Rose his wife
	Feb. 17.	Elizabeth Wiseman daughter to John Wiseman and Elizabeth his wife
1600.	June 18.	Olyver Emans sonne unto George Emans and Dyonis his wife
	Jan. 18.	Bridget Johnson daughter of Thomas Johnson and Elizabeth his wife
1601.	April 30.	Margrette Seppens daughter of ffrancis Seppens and Margret his wife
1602.	Aug. 24.	Roger Alden sonne of John Alden and Emme his wife
	Jan. 6.	Steven ffoxe sonne of Edwarde ffoxe and Annys his wife
	Jan. 16.	William Seppens sonne of ffrancis Seppens and Margret his wife
	March 3.	Jane Lewes daughter of John Lewes and Rose his wife
1603.	April 10.	Jane Emans daughter of George Emans and Dionys his wife
	Feb. 11.	Rose Weast daughter of Rowlande Weast and Joane his wife
1604.	April 5.	Mary Johnson daughter of Thomas Johnson and Elizabeth his wife
	Aug. 12.	ffrancis Sargeant sonne of Bulbrooke Sargeant and Dyanis his wife
1605.	Aug. 11.	Edwarde foxe sonne of Edwarde foxe and Annys his wife
1606.	Sep. 7.	Elizabeth Lewes daughter of John Lewes and Rose his wife
	Sep. 21.	Roberte Wiseman sonne of John Wiseman and Elizabeth his wife

1607.	April 5.	Robert Browne sonne of John Browne and Mary his wife
	June 24.	Elizabeth Johnson daughter of Thomas Johnson and Elizabeth his wife
	Jan. 11.	Jane Spaldinge daughter of George Spaldinge and Sarah his wife
1608.	March 31.	Anne ffoxe daughter of Edwarde foxe and Anne his wife
	April 24.	George Seppens sonne of ffrancys Seppens and Margret his wife
1609.	May 28.	Thomas Spaldinge sone of George Spaldinge and Sarah his wife
	July 30.	Margret Kinge daughter of Nicholas Kinge and Anne his wife
	Oct. 15.	Alice Johnson daughter of Thomas Johnson and Elizabeth his wife
1610.	June 24.	John Broome sonne of John Broome and Mary his wife
	Sep. (—)	Elizabeth ffoxe daughter of Edward ffoxe and Anne his wife
1611.	May 5.	Rose Hardy daughter of Edward Hardy and Anne his wife
	Nov. 3.	Elizabeth Seppens daughter of ffrancys Seppens and Margrett his wife
1612.	Feb. 28.	Margrett Thurson daughter of John Thurson and Mary his wife
1613.	May 24.	Elizabeth ffoxe daughter of Thomas ffoxe and Elizabeth his wife
	July 7.	Elizabeth Coke daughter of Mr Arthure Coke and Elizabeth his wife *
1614.	July 3.	Thomas Wiseman sonne of John Wiseman and Elizabeth his wife

* Extract from Suckling's 'History of the Hundred of Blything, Bramfield,' p. 176:—

"*Monuments.*—In the chancel, and attached to the north wall, is a large and costly monument erected to the memory of Arthur Coke, third son of Sir Edward Coke, Lord Chief Justice, by Bridget his first wife, daughter of John Paston, Esq. In the upper compartment is a kneeling figure of the first-mentioned gentleman in a military habit, carved out of white marble, which retains its polish and freshness in a very remarkable degree. The figure possesses considerable ease, and is much superior in execution to the recumbent effigy of the female which reclines in a stiff attitude, holding an infant in her arms, on an altar-tomb at the feet of her husband. The monument is profusely charged with the armorial cognizances of Coke and Waldegrave, with various quarterings. On the first shield appears Coke, with four coats, viz.—

1. COKE.—Party per pale gules and az. 3 eagles displayed argent.
2. Arg. a chev. between 3 chaplets az. flowered or.
3. Sab. a chev. between 3 covered cups or.
4. Arg. 6 fleurs-de-lis az. 3, 2. 1. and a chief indented, or : impaling Waldegrave, of four coats.
1. WALDEGRAVE.—Party per pale arg. and gules ; a crescent sab. for difference.
2. Barry of ten, arg. and az.
3. Erm. a fess sab. between 3 rosettes or.
4. Arg. a fess between 3 mullets azure."

The inscription is as follows :—
"Here lyeth byried Arthor Coke, Esq., third sonne of Sir Edward Coke, Knight, late Lord Chiefe Jvstice of England, and of the Privye Connsell of Kinge James. Here lyeth also buried in the same tombe, Elizabeth, daughter and sole Heire Apparent of Sir George Waldegrave, Knight, w'eh Elizabeth, christianly and peaceably departed this life the 14th day of November, Anno D'ni 1627. And the said Arthor likewise christianly and peaceably departed this life at Bury St Edmunds, in this county of Suffolk, on the 6th day of December, 1629.

"They had issue betweene them, living at their deceases, foure daughters, viz.

"Elizabeth, Mary, Winifred, and Theophila, whom Almighty God prosper and protect."
The three eldest were baptized at Thorington 1613, 1615, 1621, and a daughter Bridget was buried April 2, 1622.

	July 10.	Elizabeth Nichols daughter of William Nichols and Katharine his wife
	Oct. 9.	Thomas Morse sonne of Edward Morse and Grace his wife
1615.	Aug. 13.	Dorcas Reve daughter of Thomas Reve and Elizabeth his wife
	Nov. 9.	Mary Coke daughter of Arthur Coke Esqʳ and Elizabeth his wife
1616.	March 28.	William Nicholls sonne of William Nichols and Katherine his wife
	Dec. 19.	William sonne of Edward Mosse and Grace his wife
1617.	May 4.	Elizabeth Reeve daughter of Thomas Reeve and Elizabeth his wife
1618.	May 5.	Thomas Nichols sonne of William Nichols and Katherine his wife
	March 4.	Margret Cherison daughter of John Cherison and Margrett his wife

Francis Kynnaston
Rector Ecclesie
de Thorington

(*This Signature of Francis Kynnaston testifies to his becoming Rector in 1620, though his institution is not recorded in the books of the Diocesan Registry. See "Rectors of Thorington," page 7.*)

1620.	Sep. 6.	John Rene sonne of Thomas Rene and Elizabeth his wife
	Sep. 8.	Frances Stacey daughter of James Stacy and Alice his wife
	Dec. 23.	Elizabeth Dinnington daughter of Thomas and Elizabeth
1621.	Sep. 2.	Francis Mosse daughter of Edward Mosse and Grace his wyfe
	Nov. 8.	John Nicols sonne of William Nicols and Katarine his wyfe
	Nov. 14.	Thomas feltham sonne of Harborne feltham* and Myriell his wyfe
	Dec. 9.	Mary Stacye daughter of James and Alice his wyfe
	Feb. 21.	Wynefred Coke daughter of Arthur Coke Esquire and Elizabeth his wife
1622.	Sep. 12.	ffrancis Seppens sonne of ffrancis Seppens and Margerie his wife
1623.	July 6.	Edmund Feltham sonne of Harborne Feltham and Muriell his wife [wyfe
	Oct. 10.	Ann Debenham daughter of Andrew Debenha' and Ellen his
1624.	July 25.	Johne Cleaford sone of James Cleaford and Martha his wyfe
	Oct. 3	Robert Fellow sonne of Robert Fellow and Alice his wife
	Jan. 30.	Reginald Mordock and Tobias Mordock sonnes of William Mordock and Susa' his wife [his wife
1625.	May 11.	Mary ffeltham daughter of Harborne ffeltham, gent. and Muriell his wife
	Sep. 14.	George Seppins sone of francis Seppins and Marrwrie his wife
1626.	April 30.	William Aldus sone of Richard Aldus and Mary his wife

* *Described 1625 and 1627 as "Gentleman." His children baptized at Thorington were—Thomas, 1621; buried 1622, Edmund, 1623; buried 1682. Mary, 1625; buried 1626. Margaret, 1627. He himself was buried 1638. See Registers of these dates.*

1626.	Oct. 3.	Briget Cooke daughter of Henrie Cook Esquire and Margaret his wife*
1627.	April 11.	Margaret feltame daughter of harborne feltame gentleman and Muriel his wife
	May 27.	Marye Clifforde daughter of James Clifford and Martha his wife
	Sep. 9.	Margaret daughter of Francis Seppens and Margery his wife
	Sep. 25.	Elizabeth daughter of John ffreman, Clarke, and Elizabeth his wife†
1628.	April 28.	Jane Cooke daughter of Henry Coke Esquire and Margaret his wife and she was borne ye 4^d of Aprill An'o pred
	Jan. 21.	Marye daughter of Richard Aldus and Mary his wife
1629.	July 23.	Margaret daughter of Samuel Garrould and Margaret his wife
	Aug. 24.	Robert sone of Henrie Coke Esquire and Margaret his wife
	Jan. 3.	Henrye sone of Richard Aldus and Marye his wife
	Sep. 16.	Parnell daughter of Steven Pilburrow and Elizabeth his wife
1630.	June 20.	Richard son' of James Presson and Elizabeth his wife
	June 20.	Parnell daughter of John Tocklye and Rose his wife
	Sep. 3.	William son'e of Samuel Garrould and Margaret his wife
	Oct. 27.	Thomas son'e of Henrye Coke Esquire and Margaret his wife
	Dec. 9.	Raynold sonne of Raynold Lenys and ffrancis his wife
1631.	July 31.	James sonne of Gualter and ffrancis Pilbourough
	Oct. 6.	John sonne of James and Elizabeth Preston
	Jan. 22.	Margaret daughter of Richard and Marye Aldus
1632.	April 14.	Theophilah daughter of Henrye and Margaret Coke Esq.
	Nov. 18.	Richard sonne of Nicholas Rumsby and Grace his wife
	Nov. 22.	John sonne of ffrancis Seppens and Margery his wife
	Jan. 5.	Elizabeth daughter of John Tockly and Rose his wife

* Extract from Johnson's 'Life of Sir Edward Coke,' pp. 397, 398 :—

Henry (*fifth son of Sir Ed. Coke*), who was baptized at Huntingfield, August 30, 1592 (*The Huntingfield Register gives* 1591), was seated at Thurrington in Norfolk (*mistake for Suffolk*). He was elected member of Parliament in 1623 for Wycomb, twice in 1625 for the same borough, and in 1640 for Dunwich. He married Margaret, daughter and heiress of Edward Lovelace, by whom he had a son Richard, who espoused Mary, daughter of Sir John Rous, Bart., their son Robert (*only son—Suckling's 'Suffolk'*) succeeded, on the death of John Coke (*4th son of Sir E. Coke*), to the Holkham estates and the greatest part of Sir Edward Coke's property.

His children, baptized at Thorington, were : 1. *Briget. Oct. 3, 1626.* 2. *Jane, Ap. 28, 1628 ;* buried March 3, 1642-3. 3. *Robert, Aug. 24, 1629 ; buried Dec. 21, 1630.* 4. *Thomas, Oct. 27, 1630 ; buried April 19, 1631.* 5. *Theophilah, April 14, 1632.* 6. *Robert, Nov. 27, 1634 ; buried Dec. 28, 1661.*

Henry Coke was buried Nov. 19, 1661, and his son Cyriack Coke Aug. 2, 1679. See Registers at those dates.

Extract from Suckling's ' Suffolk,' pp. 367, 369 :—

Mary, daughter of Sir John Rous, by Elizabeth daughter of Sir Christopher Yelverton [sister of Sir John Rous of Henham Hall, created Bart. 1660], married Richard Coke, Esq., of Thorington, grandson of the celebrated Sir Edward Coke, the only son of which marriage inherited the Holkham estates, upon failure of the male descendants of John Coke, Esq., who died at Honington, in Suffolk, in 1661 [Blomefield, art. Holkham].

† (*Elizabeth, wife of John ffreeman, Clark, was buried this same day Sept. 25, 1627, and John freman, Clarke, March 22, 1656. See Registers at those dates.*)

E

1632.	Jan. 31.	Abigal daughter of Phylip Godbold and Abigal his wife
	Feb. 3.	Margaret daughter of William Seppens and Mary his wife
1633.	July 25.	Theophylah daughter of Nathaniell Duckett and Margaret his wife
	Feb. 16.	Katharine daughter of ffrancis Burward and Maye his wife
1634.	July 10.	Marye daughter of William and Prudence Cone
	Nov. (—)	Elizabeth daughter of William and Elizabeth Groome
	Nov. 27.	Robert sonne of Henrye and Margaret Coke Esq.
	Feb. 20.	ffrancis sonne of Richard and Mary Aldus
1635.	April 27.	Philip sone of Phylip Godbold and Abigal his wife
	April 27.	Jane daughter of James and Elizabeth Presson
	Dec. 6.	Katharine daughter of James and Elizabeth Presson
1636.	Oct. 9.	Thomas sonne of William and Prudence Cone
	Jan. 5.	Jane daughter of Richard and Marye Aldus
1637.	March 26.	Sarah daughter of James and Elizabeth Presson
	Jan. 28.	Anne daughter of Jermiah and Anne Stannard
1638.	July 8.	Margaret daughter of William and Prudence Cone
	Sep. 9.	John sonne of Robt. and Anne Brown
1639.	May 12.	James sonne of James and Elizabeth Presson
	Dec. 21.	ffrances daughter of William and Anne ffreeman
	Jan. 26.	Margaret daughter of William and Elizabeth Groome
1640.	Sep. 6.	ffrancis and Anne son' and daughter of Robt. and Anne Browne
1641.	May 30.	Anne Durrente daughter of John Durrente and Anne his wiue
	June. 3.	Willm. son of Willm. freman and Anne his wiue
	Aug. 6.	Thom. and Alse son and daughter of Thomas Scotte and Katheren his wiue
	Sep. 19.	Elizabeth daughter of Robt. Browne and Ann his wiue
1642.	May 20.	Margaret daughter of Ham'ond Douty and [blank] his wife
1643.	March 3.	Joh. sone of Joh. and Anne Durrant
1644.	May 16.	Margaret Seppence daughter of George and Margaret Seppence
1643.*	Feb. 15.	Ann daughter of James and Margaret Preston
	June 16.	Vere daughter of Tho. and ffrances ffiske
1644.	Jan. 9.	Joh. son'e of Joh. and Elizabeth Deues
1645.	July 27.	Tho. son'e of Tho. and ffrances ffiske
	March 15.	Nicholas son'e of ffrancis and Mathye Clarke

Francis Seppings beinge chosen & suorne Register for ye Parish of Thorington accordinge to a late Act of Parliament dated 24th of August 1653 was allowed & approoved by us this 21th of Octob. 1653.†

                       J. BREWSTER.

                       SAM. FFAWETHER.

* *This and several others dated in the following pages are misplaced in these Registers, but the entries are copied as they are placed, as exemplifying the habits of our clerical ancestors.*

† An abstract of the Act of Parliament passed August 25, 1653, concerning Marriages and the registering thereof, and also of Births and Burials :—

It was enacted, " That all Persons in England or Ireland, intending to be married, should, twenty one days at least before, deliver in Writing to the Register appointed by this Act for the Parish where each Party to be married live, with their Names, Surnames, Additions, and Places

1653.	Dec. 8.	Margret daughter of francis Sepenes and Matha his wife
	Feb. 1.	Edmond son of John Dorente and Mary his wife
	Feb. 5.	Matha daughter of Robt. felloe and Mary his wife
	Feb. 19.	Johon son of francis Collet and Anne his wife
1654.	April 14.	Willam sone of Willam Honner and Elizabeth his wife
	Nov. 5.	Marcy daughter of John Dorant and Margret his wife

of Abode, and of their Parents, Guardians, or Overseers ; all which the said Register shall publish three several Lord's Days then next following, at the close of the Morning Exercise, in the Church or Chapel : or, if the Parties to be married desired it, in the Market-Place next adjoining thereto, on three Market-Days, in three several Weeks next following, between the hours of Eleven and Two ; which being done, the Register shall, upon request of the Parties concerned, make a certificate of the due performance thereof, without which such Marriage shall not proceed : And if any exception be made thereto, the Register shall insert the same, with the Name of the Person making such exception, and their Place of Abode, in the Certificate of Publication.

"All Persons intending to be married, shall come before some Justice of Peace of the same County, City, or Town Corporate, where Publication hath been made, and bring a Certificate thereof, with proof of the consent of their Parents or Guardians, if either of the Parties be under the age of twenty-one years : And the Justice shall examine, upon oath, concerning the truth of the certificate, and due performance of all the Premises, and of any exception arising ; and, if there be no reasonable cause to the contrary, the Marriage shall proceed in this manner :

"The Man, taking the Woman by the hand, shall distinctly pronounce these words, *I A.B. do here in the presence of God, the Searcher of all Hearts, take thee C.D. for my wedded Wife ; and do also in the presence of God, and before these Witnesses, promise to be unto thee a loving and faithful Husband.*

"And then the Woman, taking the Man by the hand, shall also distinctly pronounce these words, *I C.D. do here in the presence of God, the Searcher of all Hearts, take thee A.B. for my wedded Husband ; and do also in the presence of God, and before these Witnesses, promise to be unto thee a loving, faithful, and obedient Wife.*

"The Man and Woman having made sufficient proof of the consent of their Parents or Guardians, and expressed their consent to Marriage, in the manner and words aforesaid, before such Justice of Peace, in the presence of two or more credible witnesses, he shall declare them to be from thenceforth Husband and Wife ; and after such consent so expressed, and such declaration made, the same shall be good and effectual in law ; and no other Form of Marriage shall be accounted valid according to the Laws of England. But the Justice of Peace, in case of dumb persons, may dispense with pronouncing the words aforesaid ; and with joining hands, in case of persons that have no hands.

"A Book of Vellum or Parchment shall be provided for the registering of all such Marriages, and of all Births of Children, and Burials of all sorts of People, within every Parish ; for the safe keeping of which the Inhabitants and Householders, chargeable to the poor, shall make choice of some able and honest person, to be approved by one Justice of the Peace of the County, and so signified under his hand in the said Register Book, to have the keeping thereof, who shall therein enter all such Publications, Marriages, Births of Children, and Burials of all sorts of Persons, and the Names of every of them, and the Days of the Month and Year thereof, and the Parents, Guardians, or Overseers' Names ; and for such Publications and Certificate, the Register shall be paid 1s., also 1s. for the entry of every Marriage ; for every Birth of a Child 4d., and for every Death 1d. But for Publications, Marriages, Births, or Burials of poor people, who live upon alms, nothing shall be taken. And the Justice of Peace, if desired, shall give a Certificate on Parchment, under his Hand and Seal, of such Marriage, and of the Day of the Solemnization thereof, and of two or more of the Witnesses then present. for which his Clerk to receive 1s. And if such Certificate shall be produced to the Clerk of the Peace for that County, and request made to him to make an Entry thereof, he shall enter the same in a Book of Parchment to be provided for that purpose, and kept amongst the Records of the said Sessions, for which he may receive 4d.

1654.	Nov. 19.	Anne daughter of John Collet and Elizabeth his wife
	Feb. 1.	Sara daughter of Willam Sampson and Sara his wife
1655.	April 25.	Thomas son of Thomas Scotte and frances his wife
	June 4.	Thomas son of John Deanes and Elizabeth his wife
	June 21.	Susana daughter of Robrt. Batman and Susana his wife
	July 5.	Alaxander son of John Dvrante and Mary his wife
	Sep. 16.	Mary, and Matha davghteres of ffrancis Seppenes and Matha his wife
	Oct. 26.	Anne davghter of Thomas fiske and frances his wife
	Nov. 1.	Margret davghter of Willam Larke and Margret his wife
1656.	May 1.	Elizabeth davghter of Robrt. Gurllinge and Mary his wife
	Sep. 2.	Sara davghter of Robert Bloweres and Grace his wife
1657.	May 4.	francis son of Thomas Scott and frances his wif
	June 21.	Margret davghter of Robt. Gurllinge and Mary his wife
	Aug. 29.	Robert son of Robert Batman and Sysan his wife
1659.	Dec. 10.	Anne daghter of Robrte Blloweres and Grace his wife
	Jan. 9.	Anes daghter of John Durant and Margret his wife
1660.	Feb. 3.	Willam son of Willam Cone and Rose his wife
1661.	Jan. 9.	Mary davghter of Allaxander Dvrant and Marye his wife
	Jan. 16.	Gorge son of ffrancis Seppenes and Matha his wife
[1667?]	Jan. 10.	Edmund sonne of Edmund Rabett* and Frances his wife [*Edmund bur. 1680—Francis, widdow, bur. 1682.]
1667.	Jan. 25.	Bridgett daughter of John Miller and Elizabeth his wife
1676.	Jan. 26.	Mary daughter of John Taylor and Ciscella his wif
1672.	May 24.	Judah daughter of William and Mary Blowers
1675.	Dec. 27.	John sonne of John and Elizabeth Lambe
	June 30.	John sonne of William and Mary Blowers

"If any Person shall, by Violence or Fraud, steal or take away any one under the age of 21 years, or cause so to be done, with intent of Marriage, he shall forfeit his whole Estate, Real and Personal; one-half to the Commonwealth, and the other to the Party so taken away; and farther suffer close imprisonment, and to be kept to hard labour in some House of Correction during life: and every Person convicted of aiding or abetting any such Violence or Fraud, shall be imprisoned and kept to hard labour for the space of seven years; and any pretended Marriage obtained by such Violence and Fraud, shall be null and void.

"Where any Guardian shall betray his trust touching any Child, by seducing, selling, or otherwise wilfully putting such Child into the hands or power of any Person to marry such Child, without his or her free consent, such Guardian shall forfeit double the Value of such Child's portion, one moiety thereof to the Commonwealth, and the other to the Child so married.

"The Age for a Man to consent unto Marriage shall be 16 years, and the age of a Woman 14 years.

"Controversies touching Contracts and Marriages to be determined at the General Quarter Sessions of the Peace."—'Parliamentary History of England to the Restoration of Car. II.,' 2nd Edition, Vol. xx., p. 214, 1763.

* "The [Rabett] family is said to be of Norman extraction, and has been connected with Suffolk for at least four hundred years. Willielmus Rabett occurring as Member in Parliament for Dunwich in 1467. In 1562, Henry and Anthony Denny, Esqrs., alienated to Reginald Rabett and his heirs certain estates in Bramfield; and in the 14th of Elizabeth, Walter Norton, Esq., sold divers lands, tenements, and hereditaments to Reginald Rabett, gentleman, in Bramfield, Thorington, Darsham, and Hinton."—Suckling's 'Suffolk,' Bramfield, p. 172.

Bramfield Hall and estate are still in the possession of the Rabett family.—T. S. H.

1670.	March 19.	Elizabeth daughter of John and Elizabeth Miller
1674.	Sep. 6.	John sonne of John and Elizabeth Miller
1676.	Nov. 17.	Benjamen sonne of John and Elizabeth Miller
1677.	Jan. 30.	Anne daughter of ffrancis Taylor and Anne his wife
1678.	March 25.	Mary daughter of John Mayhew,* Clerk, and Anne his wife
	July 19.	Margret daughter of Robert and [blank] Blowers
	Sep. 2.	George sonne of John and Matthew Evans
	Sep. 1.	Anne-ffella Base daughter of Anne Smith [*The first "base" born child since* 1561.]
	Oct. 25.	Elizabeth daughter of John Lambe and Elizabeth his wife
	Dec. 15.	Oliue [*buried* 23 *Dec^r*] and Rebekah [*buried* 28 *Dec^r*] daughters of Hermon and Rebekah Attwood†
	Jan. 13.	Mary daughter of Thomas and Alice Moore
1679.	Dec. 5.	Anne daughter of John Wade and Mercie his wife
	Feb. 27.	Rose daughter of Georg and Alice Ballard
1680.	Oct. 7.	Laurence sonne of John Mayhew, Clerk, and Anne his wife
	Feb. 9.	Martha daughter of Robert and Margret Smith
1681.	April 3.	Mathew daughter of Robert and Susanna ffella
	Nov. 10.	Elizabeth Base child of Cherry Thirston born at Bramfield
1682.	April 9.	William sonne of John and Elizabeth Lambe
	Sep. 6.	John sonne of John Wade and Mercy his wife
	Sep. 24.	William sonne of William and Mary Blowers
	Dec. 17.	Willm sonne of William and Margret Taylor
	Jan. 12.	Willm sonne of John and Elizabeth Miller
	Feb. 14.	Thomas sonne of Thomas Scott and Elizabeth his [blank]
	March 5.	Benjamen Base sonne of Matthew Evans widdow
1683.	May 2.	William sonne of William and Sarah Browne

* *John Mayhew, Rector* 1676 (*see Institutions*); *Rector of Holton,* 1687-8; *buried in the Churchyard,* 1693, *M.I. His widow, Ann, bur.* 1721, *M.I. Children mentioned in these Registers :* —*Mary, bap.* 1678 ; *Thomas, bur.* 1680 ; *Laurence, bap. and bur.* 1680 ; *Anne, bap. and bur.* 1683 ; *Katherine, bap.* 1684 ; *Thomas, bap. and bur.* 1688.

† The name Attwood does not occur again in these Registers, except at the burial of these children in December of this year. Coupled with the Christian names Hermon and Olive it possesses interest. In a short account of the " Manor of Sanderstead," co. Surrey, by Granville Leveson Gower, Esq., published by Wyman and Sons, 1878, is the following notice, pp. 3, 4 :—

"John Ownstead . . . . died on the 9th August, 1600, aged sixty-six, and was buried in Sanderstead Church. . . . . Leaving no issue, he by his will devised this manor, after the death of his second wife Margaret, to his cousin Harmon Atwood.

"The family of Attwood, of whom a pedigree is given by Manning [' Hist. of Surrey,' vol. ii., p. 570], had long been seated at Sanderstead, and were, I imagine, a yeoman family of the place. In a fine of land relating to Sanderstead, 19 Ed. III., I find the name of Peter Atte Wood, and in Coulsdon, the adjoining parish, the same name occurs in 6 Ed. II., when Peter at Wode, John and Roger de Bosco [or of the Wood,] are returned as owning lands in that parish : . . . .

"Harman Atwood died in 1653, aged eighty-three, as appears by the inscription on his monument in the Church. . . . . After him we find his fourth son, Harman Atwood, in possession, and he by his will devised Sanderstead to his brother John and his sister Olive for their lives, with remainder to Harman Atwood, son of his elder brother John."

[*The Christian names Harman and Olive seem to imply a connection between the Thorington and Sanderstead families.*]

1683.	Aug. 30.	Anne daughter of John Mayhew, Clerke, and Anne his wife
	Jan. 2.	Lucy daughter of John and Lucy Agur
1684.	Nov. 11.	Katherine daughter of John Mayhew, Clerke, and Anne his wife
	Jan. 9.	Abraham sonne of William and Mary Blowers
	Jan. 2.	ffrancis sonne of John and Anne Bird
1685.	Nov. 25.	John sonne of John and Lucy Agur
	Dec. 1.	John sonne of William and Sarah Browne
1686.	April 4.	Joseph sonne of Elizabeth Lambe
	Dec. 13.	*Mary dafter of To Scockt and Elizebeth his wife
1689.	Aug. 27.	•Tho son of Tho Scockt and Elizebth his wife
1691.	Dec. 3.	*franses son of tho Scockt and Elizeb his wife
1696.	Sep. 22.	*Elizebth dafter of Tho Scockt and Elizebth his wife
1687.	Oct. 19.	Georg sonne of William and Sarah Browne
	Oct. 21.	Sarah daughter of William and Mary Blowers
1688.	July (—)	Thomas sonne of John Mayhew, Cler., and Anne his wife
	Jan. 17.	William sonne of John and Anne Bird
	Aug. (—)	Alisebeth davgter Thomas Laison and Mary his wif
1689.	July 29.	Richard son of John & Elizabeth Lamb
169 .	March 12.	Ann davghter of Thomas Laison and Mary his wif
1692.	Dec. 20.	Daniel son of Samuel Strowger and Elizabeth his wife
1693.	Sep. 14.	William son of John and Elizabeth Lamb
1694.	Jan. 7.	Samuel son of Samuel Strowger and Elizabeth his wife
1695.	Sep. 1.	Thomas son of ffrancis Watlin and Elizabeth his wife
	Nov. 15.	Elizabeth daughter of Richard Turner and ffrances his wife
1696.	Sep. 20.	Mary daughter of ffrancis Watlin and Elizabeth his wife
	Oct. 2.	Elizabeth daughter of Thomas Scot and Elizabeth his wife
	March 21.	William son of Thomas Layston labourer† and Mary his wife
1697.	July 20.	Mary daughter of Richard Turner and ffrances his wife
	Oct. 27.	Elizabeth daughter of John Pallant and Mary his wife
1698.	May 4.	Ann daughter of Francis Watling and Eliz : his wife
	July 17.	William son of William How and Margaret his wife
	Nov. 23.	Jonathan son of John Pallant
1699.	Aug. 2.	ffrances daughter of Richard Turner and ffrances his wife
	Oct. 20.	Hannah daughter of Thomas Layston and Mary his wife
	Nov. 24.	Eliz : daughter of John Pallant
	Dec. 13.	Benjamin son of John Miller
	March 9.	Martha daughter of Tho Scot
1700.	May 12.	Hannah daughter of Robt Brown
	June 30.	Hannah daughter of Francis Watling and Eliz. his wife
1701.	April 1.	Mary daughter of John Miller
	Sep. 22.	Sarah daughter of Thomas Layson
	July 27.	John son of John Brown

* *These four Baptisms are interpolated among the Burials of the above dates evidently by one who had no authority to make entries, and they prove what the pages of the Registers at this date indicate, that in the latter years of Mr. Mayhew's incumbency (he died 1693) there was carelessness in making the entries. The Baptism of Elizabeth is entered in its proper year 1696, but the day of the month is different.*

† *First mention of employment.*

1701.	May 5.	Sarah daughter of John Pallant
1702.	Aug. 3.	John son of John Miller
	Oct. 17.	Mary daughter of Edward Darby
170⅔.	Feb. 17.	Hugo son of John Jex
1703.	Sep. 19.	Robᵗ son of John Brown
170¾.	Jan. 30.	John son of Thomas Layson
	Jan. 31.	Eliz daughter of John Miller
1704.	July 16.	Ann daughter of Eliz : Lewis
	March 27.	Rebecca daughter of ffrancis Watlin labourer
	July 27.	Ann daughter of Stephen Sewell
1706.	Dec. 17.	Samuell son of John Miller
	June 24.	William son of William Pepper
1707.	Dec. 17.	John son of Stephen Sewell
1708.	Jan. 27.	Eliz. daughter of Will Goodall
1709-10.	Jan. 8.	Elizebeth daughter of Tho. Clark
1710.	Oct. 22.	Joⁿ son of Joⁿ and Mary French
1710-1.	Jan. 8.	William son of John Miller
1708.	Oct. 18.	Susan daughter of John Miller
1710-11.	Jan. 28.	Margarett daughter of John and Eliz. Coppin
1711.	May 6.	Thomas son of Thomas and Elizebeth Clark
1711-12.	March 16.	Thomas son of John and Mary French
1712.	March 30.	Henry son of John and Mary Miller
	Dec. 28.	James son of Tho. Cook and Ann his wife
1713.	April 1.	Ann daughter of Thomas Clark and Elizebeth his wife
1714.	June 9.	Bridgett daughter of John Miller and Mary his wife
1715.	April 3.	John son of William Lamb
	Sep. 22.	Mary daughter of Tho. Clark and Elizebeth his wife
1715-16.	Jan. 25.	Sarah daughter of John Miller and Mary his wife
1716.	May 16.	Elizebeth daughter of Gregory Adams and Elizebeth his wife
1716-17.	March 15.	Henry son of John Miller and Mary his wife
1721.	June 22.	Elizabeth daughter of John Watlin and Sarah his wife
	Nov. 5.	Thomas son of Thomas Cole and Ann his wife
1722.	Dec. 2.	Edward son of William Burward and Mary his wife
	Dec. 23.	William son of John Baxter and Anne his wife
1722-3.	Feb. 27.	Margett daughter of John Wattlin and Sarah his wife
1723.	Sep. 29.	Charles son of Robert and Mary Agur
	Dec. 22.	Elizebeth daughter of Tho. Cole and Anne his wife
1723-4.	Dec. 26.	Robert son of Will. Harvey and Anne his wife
1724-5.	Dec. 26.	Anne daughter of Will. Harvey and Anne his wife
1725.	May 30.	Thomas son of James Barker
	Sep. 12.	William son of William Ellis and Mary his wife
	Oct. 24.	Anne daughter of Tho. Cole and Anne his wife
	Dec. 3.	Margaret ... of William and Mary Burward
1725-6.	Dec. 26.	William son of William Harvy and Anne his wife
1726.	July 3.	Margaret daughter of William and Margaret Estaugh
	Nov. 6.	Thomas son of John Baxter and Anne his wife
1727.	March 27.	Elizebeth daughter of Wᵐ Harvy and Anne his wife

1727.	Aug. 24.	John son of John Watlin and Sarah his wife
	Sep. 24.	William . . . of Thomas and Mary Rimington
1727-8.	March 5.	Sarah daughter of Wm Harvy and Anne his wife
1728.	Aug. 18.	Robert . . . of William and Margaret Estangh
1728-9.	Jan. 17.	Anne daughter of Thomas Haddenham and Anne his wife
	Feb. 23.	Thomas son of Thomas Rymmington and Mary his wife
1729.	April 6.	Mary daughter of James Tuttle and Elizebeth his wife of ye parish of Blyborow
	May 11.	Thomas Base son of Thomas Bliss and Sarah Meen
	Oct. 5.	Elizebeth daughter of John Spooner and Margett his wife
1729-30.	Feb. 22.	Susan ye Base Child of John Adams and Mary Crisp
	Feb. 25.	Philip son of Philip Stowger and Jane his wife
1730.	April 3.	Sarah of Thomas and Anne Cole
	May 3.	Elizebeth daughter of George Berry and Elizebeth his wife
	May 31.	Sarah daughter of Thomas Rymmington and Mary his wife
1731.	June 24.	Daniell son of George Berry and Elizebeth his wife
	Feb. 23.	Elizebeth daughter of Philip Stroger and Jane his wife
1732.	April 16.	Rebecca daughter of Tho. Cole and Anne his wife
	April 23.	Henry son of Joⁿ Stroger and Eliz. his wife
1732-3.	Jan. 21.	James son of James Stroger and Susan his wife
1733.	Oct. 15.	Samuell son of Sam^{ll} Studd and Hanah his wife
1733-4.	Jan: 4.	Daniell son of George Berry and Elizebeth his wife
	Jan. 31.	Catherine daughter of Henry Brown and Eliz. his wife
1734.	May 12.	Robert son of Christopher Jarvis and Sarah his wife
	June 14.	Elizebeth daughter of Thomas Rymmington and Mary his wife
	July 5.	Elizebeth daughter of Edward Tyrrell and Eliz. his wife
	Aug. 4.	Mary daughter of Joⁿ Spooner and Margett his wife
1734-5.	Jan. 19.	Henry son of Henry Brown and Elizebeth his wife
1735.	June 29.	Rebecca daughter of Tho. Cole and Anne his wife
1735-6.	Jan. 29.	Elizebeth daughter of Henry Brown and Elizebeth his wife
1736.	April 4.	Hannah daughter of Sam^{ll} Studd and Hannah his wife
	May 2.	Sarah daughter of Tho. Rymmington and Mary his wife
	July 5.	Henry son of John Stroger and Elizibeth his wife
	Oct. 8.	Sarah daughter of Sam^{ll} Harvy and Sarah his wife
	Oct. 10.	Susan daughter of Edward Tyrrell
1737.	Oct 2.	Mary daughter of Christopher and Sarah Jarvice
	Oct. 23.	Mary daughter of Thomas Youngs and Elizabeth Spooner base born
1738.	June 2.	Robert son of John and Hannah Riches
	Jan. 12.	Henry son of Henry and Eliz. Brown
1739.	April 22.	Robert of Robert and Eliz. Spore.* Rec'd into ye Church May 13th
	May 26.	Philip of Philip and Jane Stroger, privately. Rec'd into ye Church June 14.
	Nov. 4.	John of John and Lydia Solomon was wholly baptiz'd
	Nov. 25.	William of Samuel and Hannah Studd priv. Rec^d into ye Church Jan. 18.

First notice of private baptism in this Register.

1739.	Jan. 21.	Sarah of Christopher and Sarah Jarves
1740.	May 1.	John of Edward and Eliz. Tyrrell
	June 1.	Elizebeth of John and Eliz. Baxter was publickly baptiz'd*
	Aug. 17.	Thomas of John and Ann Aldred privately. Receiv'd into Church Sep. 14
1741.	June 24.	William of Robert and Elizabeth Spore
	July 12.	Rebecka daughter of Nathaniel and Judah Esther
	Aug. 9.	John of Edward and Elizabeth Tyrrell privately
	Sep. 13.	Lydia daughter of John and Lydia Solomon
	Dec. 30.	John son of Edward Tirrell and Elizabeth his wife
1741-2.	Jan. 19.	Sarah daughter of Henry Coates and Mary his wife
1742.	Aug. 29.	Sarah daughter of Samuel Studd and Hannah his wife
1743.	May 22.	Lydia daughter of John and Lydia Solomon
1744-5.	March 10.	Sarah daughter of Christopher and Sarah Jarves
1745.	June 30.	Francis son of Francis and Elizabeth Docking
	Sep. 29.	Samuel son of Samuel Harvey and Sarah his wife
1746.	May 17.	James son of Philip and Jane Stronger privately
	Dec. 14.	Elizabeth daughter of Samuel Studd and Hannah his wife
1747.	Aug. 29.	Sarah daughter of Francis and Elizabeth Docking privately
1748.	April 22.	William son of John and Elizabeth Knoller privately
	Aug. 3.	Margaret daughter of Samuel Harvy and Sarah his wife
	Oct. 11.	John son of Francis and Elizabeth Docking, receiv'd into Church Jan. 20.
1749.	July 23.	Ann daughter of Richard and Ann Woodgate privately, rec'd into Church Sep. 25
1749-50.	Mar. 18.	John son of Francis and Elizabeth Doking privately
1750.	Sep. 25.	Richard son of Richard and Ann Woodgate
	Oct. 5.	Ann daughter of Samuel and Hannah Studd
	Oct. 7.	William son of Samuel and Sarah Harvy privately, receiv'd into Church Oct. 22
	Sep. 15.	Susannah daughter of William Carvr and Susannah his wife privately, receiv'd into Church Sep. 17, 1751
1751.†	Sep. 29.	Elizabeth daughter of Richard and Ann Woodgate

* *This expression frequently recurs, but I do not repeat it. I insert "privately" and "rec^d into Church" because it shews the child to have been alive at two different dates.*—T. S. H.

† Until A.D. 1751 the year was reckoned as commencing on March 25 and ending on March 24, but as this usage differed from the computation employed in Scotland and neighbouring nations, and was the cause of great inconvenience in the dates of deeds and other legal writings, an Act of Parliament was then passed that the first day of January should in future be the first day of the new year, so that 1752 should commence on that day instead of on March 25. And at the same time it was enacted that (as the reckoning of time was erroneous, and there was a difference of eleven days between the reckoning of the equinoxes and their recurrence), that number of eleven days should be struck out of the calendar, so that the day "following the second day of September shall be called, reckoned, and accounted to be the fourteenth day of September." At the same time it was also further enacted, "that for the continuing and preserving the calendar or method of reckoning, and computing the days of the year in the same regular course, as near as may be, in all times coming," "the several years of our Lord, 1800, 1900, 2100, 2200, 2300, or any other hundredth years of our Lord, which shall happen in time to come, except only every fourth hundredth year of our Lord, whereof the year of our Lord 2000 shall be

F

1753.	March 16.	Elizabeth daughter of Samuel and Sarah Harvy
	June 7.	Jonathan son of Richard and Ann Woodgate privately
	Oct. 12.	John son of John and Sarah Botwright
1754.	Jan. 20.	William son of William and Susannah Carvr
	March 31.	Elizabeth daughter of Rob[t] and Elizabeth Hitcham privately
	Sep. 22.	William son of William and Mary Woodyard
1755.	Jan. 5.	Elizabeth daughter of James and Elizabeth Alp
	Aug. 16.	William son of Richard and Ann Woodgate
	Dec. 14.	Sarah daughter of James and Elizabeth Alp
1756.	Jan. 4.	John son of William and Mary Woodyard
	April 19.	Esther daughter of Richard and Ann Woodgate
	Aug. 22.	Sarah base daughter of Sarah Harvy
1757.	March 18.	Sarah daughter of James and Sarah Garwood
	May 8.	John son of John and Elizabeth Goddard
	Aug. 28.	Benjamin son of William and Mary Woodyard
	Oct. 23.	William son of Henry and Hannah Briggs
1758.	Jan. 19.	William son of Henry and Hannah Briggs
	Feb. 17.	Belinda daughter of Rich[d] and Anne Woodgate
	Sep. 9.	Eliz. daughter of M[r] Tho[s] Turner* and Mary his wife
1759.	June 4.	Robert son of Rob[t] and Margaret Spore Junior
	Aug. 1.	Henry son of Henry and Hannah Briggs
	Oct. 14.	James of William and Mary Woodyard
1760.	Feb. 10.	Mary daughter of Nath[l] and Esther Harman
	April 6.	Susannah of Rich[d] and Ann Woodgate
	April 7.	Rob[t] of Robert and Sarah Churchyard
	July 8.	Eliz. of Rob[t] and Margaret Spore
1761.	March 20.	Sarah base of Sarah Rimmington
	Sep. 6.	Sarah of Rob and Margaret Spore. Receiv'd Dec. 25
	Dec. 25.	Elizabeth of William and Mary Woodyard
1762.	Jan. 3.	Ann of James and Mary Canham
	Feb. 7.	Rob[t] of Henry and Hannah Briggs privately
	Feb. 21.	William son of William and Sarah Goddard
	May 2.	Charles son of Charles and [blank] Kemp
	Dec. 5.	Robert of Rob[t] and Margaret Shade
	May 15.	Talbott son of M[r] Thomas Turner and Mary his wife
	Dec. 26.	Eliz. of Peter and Elizabeth Wichenton
1763.	March 20.	Hannah daughter of Henry and Hannah Briggs bapt. priv.
	April 3.	William of Rob[t] and Margaret Spore [Easter Day.]
	Oct. 9.	Mary daught[r] of William and Mary Woodyard

the first, shall not be esteemed to be bissextile or leap years, but shall be taken to be common years, consisting of 365 days, and no more; and that the years of our Lord, 2000, 2400, 2800, and every other fourth hundred year of our Lord, from the said year of our Lord 2000 inclusive, and also all other years of our Lord, which by the present supputation are esteemed to be bissextile or leap years, shall for the future, and in all time to come, be esteemed to be bissextile or leap years, consisting of 366 days, in the same sort and manner as is now used with respect to every fourth year of our Lord."—'The Statutes at Large,' Pickering, vol. xx., p. 186.

* Tho[s] Turner was Churchwarden "for y[e] parsonage" 1759-1784.

1763.	Nov. 20.	Margaret of Samuel and Sarah Elmy
1765.	March 31.	Elisabeth daughter of Henry and Hannah Briggs
	April 21.	Susan base child of Sarah Rimmington
	May 5.	Sarah of Nath¹ and Esther Harman
	July 7.	Margaret of Robert and Margaret Spore
1766.	Feb. 9.	James of James and Jemima Newson
	April 6.	Mary of Henry and Hannah Briggs
	July 20.	Elizabeth of Nathaniel and Esther Harman
	Aug. 31.	Robert of Robert and Mary Mitcham
1767.	March 4.	2ⁿᵈ, Willᵐ of Robᵗ and Margaret Spore
	Jan. 23.	1ˢᵗ, John of John and Elizabeth Clarke
		N.B. This last was baptised by Mʳ Leman of Wenhaston and not communicated to me till recᵈ which was June 7ᵗʰ
	July 19.	Jonathan of James and Jemima Newson
1768.	Jan. 31.	Robert of Robert and Margaret Shade
	July 24.	John of Robᵗ and Margaret Spore
	Sep. 25.	Samuel of Nathan¹ and Esther Harman
	Oct. 23.	Robert of Robert and Margaret Shade
	Nov. 11.	Mary of Sam¹ and Sarah Elmy
1769.	July 9.	Elisabeth of Henry and Hannah Briggs
	Dec. 31.	Millecent daughter of Robᵗ and Margaret Shade
	Dec. 31.	Ann [Base] of Mary Canham
1770.	Jan. 14.	William-Atkinson* [base son] of Hannah Reeve
	Sep. 18.	Thoˢ Carver of Robᵗ and Mary Butcher
	Oct. 7.	Daniel of Nath¹ and Esther Harman
1771.	Dec. 22.	Rosanna of Henry and Hannah Briggs
1772.	Feb. 7.	James of Henry and [blank] Veal
	Feb. 9.	Ann of Sam¹ and Sarah Elmy
	April 25.	William of Robert and Margaret Shade
	June 28.	William of Cornelius and Eliz. Roberts
	July 26.	Thomas of Thomas and Ann Randhall
	Oct. 25.	Joseph of Robᵗ and Mary Hitcham
1773.	April 25.	Thomas of Henry and Hannah Briggs
	May 16.	Charlotte of Wᵐ and Elisabeth Abliss
	June 13.	Elisabeth of Cornelius and Eliz. Roberts
	July 25.	Sarah of Nath¹ and Ester Harman
	Oct. 3.	Mary of Daniel and Mary Bannett
	Nov. 14.	John of Willᵐ and Martha Nolloth
1774.	July 10.	Sarah [base] of Elisabeth Studd
	Aug. 21.	Cornelius of Cornelius and Elisabeth Roberts
	Aug. 21.	James of William and Elizab. Aldoss
	Oct. 2.	Sarah of Robert and Margaret Shade
1775.	Feb. 5.	Mary of Nathan¹ and Ester Harman
	Feb. 19.	Lydia of Sam¹ and Sarah Elmy

* *The first instance of a double Christian name.*

1775.	April 30.	Walter son of W^m and Martha Nolloth
	Sep. 5.	Sarah of Danl and Mary Bunnet
	Oct. 8.	John of Henry and Hannah Briggs
	Oct. 25.	Charles* of W^m and Eliz. Aldiss
1776.	Dec. 15.	Francis son of Saml and Hannah Balls
1777.	Jan. 26.	Honoria Daug^r of W^m and Martha Nolloth
	Feb. 25.	Elisabeth* of W^m and Elisth Aldiss
	Sep. 14.	John of Robt and Marg^t Shade
1778.	Jan. 4.	Susannah of Saml and Sarah Elmy
	June 21.	Nathani(a)el of Henry and Hannah Briggs
	Oct. 25.	Willm of Willm and Martha Nolloth
	Nov. 8.	Elisabeth of [blank] and E. [blank] Fountain
1779.	July 18.	Sarah, of Peter and Ann Wickenden
	Aug. 29.	Jane of Philip and Martha Strowger
1781.	Dec. 2.	Ann of Rich^d [Jnr^r] and Sarah Woodgate
1782.	March 3.	John [base child] of [blank]
1783.	March 1.	Robert of Samuel and Sarah Elmy
	March 30	Richard of William and Sarah Knights
	July 20.	Ann of George and Sarah Nunn privately

Here end the Baptisms in the first volume.

	Oct. 26.	Jonathan son of Richard and Sarah Woodgate
1784.	March 8.	Robin son of Robert and Elizabeth Woodgate, privately, received into the Church May 23
	May 10	Lætitia daughter of Samuel Elmy and Sarah his wife (late Sarah Jarvis) was born May 5. Received into the Church, May 23
	June 6.	Ann base daughter of Elizabeth Barber was born April 8 privately
1785.	Nov. 20.	Ann daughter of William Knights and Sarah his wife (late Sarah Puttock) was born Nov. 18, 1785, privately. Rec^d into the Church Jan. 29, 1786
1786.	Jan. 15.	John son of John Smith and Mary his wife (late Mary Berry) was born Dec. 25, 1785
	Jan. 22.	Richard son of Robert Woodgate and Elizabeth his wife (late Elizabeth Moore) was born Jan. 18, privately. Received into the Church April 16
	April 2.	Charlotte daughter of William Abbet and Sarah his wife (late Sarah Coper) was born March 29
	April 9.	Mary daughter of William Girling and Sarah his wife (late Sarah Mash) was born March 17
	April 23.	Isaac son of Richard Woodgate and Sarah his wife (late Sarah Reeve) was born April 16
	Sep. 3.	Robert son of George Nunn and Sarah his wife, privately, was born Aug. 4
	Oct. 11.	Ann daughter of William Haylock and Elizabeth his wife (late Elizabeth Wickerton) was born Sep. 15

* Both received into the Church, June 25, 1787.

1786.	Oct. 29.	Sarah base daughter of Elizabeth Cooper was born Oct. 26, privately. Received into the Church Nov. 19
1787.	June 12.	Charlotte daughter of James Finch and Ann his wife (late Wickerton) was born June 11, privately
	June 28.	Thomas son of John Bullard and Sarah his wife privately, was born June 11
	Dec. 16.	Jonathan son of Robert Woodgate and Elizabeth his wife was born Dec. 7, privately. Received into the Church March 2, 1788
1788.	Jan. 13.	Elizabeth daughter of John Smith and Mary his wife (late Berry) was born Dec. 25, 1787
	Aug. 24.	Deborah daughter of William Girling and Sarah his wife (late Marsh spinster) was born Aug. 17
	Sep. 24.	Benjamin son of James Finch and Ann his wife (late Wickerton spinster) was born Sep. 23, privately. Baptized publickly May 3, 1789
	Oct. 15.	Susanna daughter of William Haylock and Elizabeth his wife (late Wickerton spinster) was born Oct. 15, privately. Received into the Church June 7, 1789
	Dec. 11.	Richard son of Geo. and Sarah Nunn (late Baxter spinster) was born Dec. 11, privately
1789.	Feb. 10.	Mary natural daughter of Mary Sayer was born July 7, 1788. Tax rec^{d*}
1790.	Jan. 24.	Mary daughter of William Knights and Sarah his wife (late Buttock spinster) was born Jan. 16. Privately. Baptized publickly March 7
	Feb. 7.	Mary daughter of John Smith and Mary his wife (late Berry spinster) was born Jan. 13
	Feb. 28.	Esther daughter of Robert Woodgate and Elizabeth his wife (late Mower spinster) was born Feb. 5, privately
	March 7.	Mary natural daughter of Deborah Marsh was born Feb. 25
	Dec. 5.	Elizabeth daughter of William Haylock and Elizabeth his wife (late Wickerton spinster) was born Nov. 30
	Dec. 5.	Sarah daughter of James Finch and Anne his wife (late Wickerton spinster) was born Oct. 29

* An Act came into operation on Oct. 1, 1783, imposing a tax of 3d. on the registration of every birth or christening, marriage, and burial. Pauper baptisms and burials were exempted. The " Parson, Vicar, or Curate " was allowed two shillings in the Pound " for his trouble," but was subject to a fine of £100 if he neglected registration. He could, however, compound for the tax by the payment of a yearly sum. This Act was considered very oppressive and vexatious and was repealed in 1794. In William the Third's reign an Act of the same kind had been in force for five years. It came into operation on May 1st, 1695. It was passed to grant his Majesty certain rates and duties on marriages, births, and burials, and upon bachelors and widowers, for the term of five years, for the carrying on of the war against France with vigour. This tax varied according to rank. On marriage from 2s. 6d. to £50 ; on births from 2s. to £30 ; on burials from 4s. to £50, and over. The tax on bachelors and widowers was a yearly one, from 1s. to £12 10s. There is no reference to the working of this Act of William's in these Registers.

1791. Jan. 23.   Mary daughter of Tall Clarke and Mary his wife (late Cable spinster) was born Jan. 11, privately

       July 23.   Susanna daughter of William Girling and Sarah his wife (late Marsh spinster) was born March 19

       Nov. 13.   John son of Thomas Warren and Mary his wife (late Smith spinster) was born Nov. 7, privately

1792. June 3.   James son of Robert Woodgate and Elizabeth his wife (late Moore spinster) was born May 4

       (——)   Anne daughter of James Finch and Ann his wife (late Wickerton spinster) was born Oct. 8

1793. June 23.   William son of William Haylock and Elizabeth his wife (late Wickerton spinster) was born April 20

       July 7.   Sarah daughter of William Girling and Sarah his wife (late Marsh spinster) was born June 13

       Aug. 11.   Marianne daughter of Thomas Lines and Elizabeth his wife (late Peake spinster) born Aug. 4, 1792, publickly (*evidently an error for privately*), rec⁴ into Church Oct. 27, 1799

1794. Jan. 5.   Elizabeth daughter of Thomas Lines and Elizabeth his wife (late Peake spinster) was born Jan. 1, privately. Rec⁴ into Church Oct. 27, 1799

       April 6.   Samuel son of Robert Woodgate and Elizabeth his wife (late Mower spinster) was born Feb. 23

       Oct. 12.   Martha daughter of John Ludbrook and Elizabeth his wife (late Strowger) was born Oct. 9, privately

1795. May 24.   Sophia daughter of James Finch and Anne his wife (late Wickerton spinster) was born Feb. 5

       April 3.   Margaret daughter of Nicolas Buckingham and Mildred his wife (late Mabson spinster) was born March 1

       June 14.   Martha daughter of John Ludbrook and Elizabeth his wife (late Strowger spinster) was born Oct. 9, 1794

       Aug. 23.   William son of William Shade and Anne his wife (late Horne spinster) was born Aug. 5, privately

       Oct. 11.   John son of William Girling and Sarah his wife was born Sep. 30, baptized privately and publickly Oct. 11, 1795

1796. Jan. 3.   Green son of William Haylock and Elizabeth his wife (late Wickerton spinster) was born Nov. 28, 1795

       March 20.   Constantine son of William Cheeston and Ann his wife (late Wade) was born March 3. Baptized privately and publickly

       June 12.   Sarah daughter of Thomas Lines and Elizabeth his wife (late Peake) was born May 24, privately

       July 17.   Elizabeth daughter of Robert Woodgate and Elizabeth his wife (late Maw) was born June 20, privately

1797. Jan. 29.   James son of Ann and James Finch born Jan. 2

       April 30.   William son of Nicholas and Mildred (late Mabson spinster) Buckingham born Feb. 11

1798. April 22.   Chester son of William and Ann (late Wade spinster) Cheston born April 15, privately

1798.	May 20.	Hannah daughter of William and Elizabeth (late Wickerton spinster) Haylock born May 18, privately
	Oct. 7.	Lydia daughter of Robert and Elizabeth (late Maw spinster) Woodgate born Sep. 30 priv. bap⁴ received into Church Nov. 10
1799.	Jan. 20.	James son of Nicholas and Mildred (late Mabson spinster) Buckingham born Dec. 30, 1798. priv. bap.
	March 10.	Rose daughter of James and Ann (late Wickerton spinster) Finch born Feb. 11
	April 28.	George son of Ann Dunnett, privately
	April 28.	John son of Judith Cooper, privately
	Oct. 27.	Wᵐ son of Thomas Lines and Elizabeth (late Peake) born Oct. 1
	Nov. 10.	Sarah daughter of Richard and Rachael Woodgate (late Wright), privately
1800.	Nov. 2.	Valentine son of Susan and Valentine Coates, privately. Received into the Church by Mʳ Badely in July 1801
1801.	Jan. 11.	James son of Wᵐ and Elizabeth Haylock (late Wickerton), priv. See below (Oct. 25th)
	March 29.	Mary daughtʳ of Mary Steggall and Robᵗ Briggs
	May 3.	Israel son of Robert Woodgate and Elizabᵗʰ (Mower) his wife
	July 19.	Phyllis daughʳ of James Finch and Ann (Wickerton) his wife
	Aug. 30.	James son of William Girling and Sarah (Marshall) his wife
	Sep. 20.	George son of Richᵈ Woodgate and Rachael (Wright) his wife
	Oct. 25.	James son of William Haylock and Elizabeth (Wickerton) his wife. Received into Church
1803.	March 20.	Geo. son of Rich. and Rachael Woodgate
	May 22.	Heley Finch born Ap. 23
	July 31.	Sarah bastard daughter of Ann Breese born 26
	Dec. 29.	William son of [blank] Smith and Elizabeth his wife (late Peak spinster) privately
1804.	Jan. 22.	Thomas son of Thomas and Elizabeth Loins (late Peak spinster) privately. Thosᵉ Lines was received in the Church May 23, 1806
	July 1.	Joseph son of Abraham and Sarah (late Smith spinster) Eastaugh at the age of 18 years and 10 months
	Dec. 2.	Mary daughter of William Shade and Ann his wife (late Horn spinster) born Nov. 1, privately
1805.	Feb. 10.	Sarah daughter of John Adams and Sarah his wife (late Wade spinster) born Jan. 28. Privately. Received in the Church May 8, 1806.
	March 24.	Hannah daughter of William Girling and Sarah his wife (late Marshall spinster) born Feb. 25
	April 12.	Ann and Betsy twin daughters of Nicholas Buckenham and Mildred his wife (late Mabson spinster), publickly. Privately March 25, 1803
	April 12.	Maria daughter of Nicholas Buckenham and Mildred his wife born Dec. 22, 1804

1805. June 2.   William son of David Smith and Martha his wife (late Martha
                Peake spinster), privately.   Received in the Church May
                22, 1806

June 2.   William son of Joseph Sporle and Mary his wife (late M. Baldry
                spinster), privately. Received in the Church May 22, 1806

June 2.   John son of Richard Woodgate and Rachel his wife (late Rachel
                Wright sp'), privately.   Received in the Church June 9

June 5.   Mary Ann daughter of Valentine Coates and Susan his wife (late
                Edwards spinster), privately. Received in the Church May
                23, 1806

1806. May 11.   Elizabeth Ann daughter of James and Ann (late Chapman)
                Aldis born May 5.   Received in the church May 22

June 29.   Susan d' of Nicholas and Mildred Buckingham (late Mabson)
                born June 3.   Received March 23, 1808

Nov. 23.   William son of Thomas and Elizabeth (late Peak) Lines born
                Nov. 18

1807. April 17. William son of James and Ann Aldis (late Chapman) priv.

April 26.   Robert son of Richard and Rachael Woodgate (late Wright)
                born Ap. 22

May 3.   William son of Robert and Ann Shields (late Horn) born May 1

July 26.   Lucy d' of William and Mary Roberts (late Girling) born July 19

Aug. 2.   Stephen son of James and Ann Long (late Winchup) born Jan.
                9, 1806. [At the bottom of this page of the Register Book
                is this memorandum, "George son of James and Ann Long
                was born Dec. 16, 1798, and received in the Church Aug.
                2, 1807;" and on the last page but one of this Register
                Book are the following entries in pencil:
                "George son of Jas. and Ann Long (late Whincup) Dec.
                16th, 1798, and rec'd Aug. 2, 1807
                "Sarah d' J. and A. L. (late W.) 3 y' old last gunpowder
                Treason."]

1806. Aug. 24. Mary Ann d' of William and Ann Scarlett (late Coultrop) born
                Aug. 19

1807. Dec. 20. Jonathan son of Jonathan and Sarah Webb (late Dale) born
                Dec. 18

1808. March 10. Sarah daughter of Joseph and Mary Spaule (late Baldry) born
                March 7

March 23.   John son of Nicholas and Mildred Buckingham (late Mabsum)
                born Jan. 3

March 27.   James son of James and Ann Aldis (late Chapman), priv. born
                March 23, 1808

May 22.   Jonathan son of James and Ann Mills (late Ann Kuights) born
                May 21, priv: bapt:

1809. April 23. Hannah daughter of Richard and Rachael Woodgate (late
                Wright) born April 16, priv. bapt.

July 16.   Jemima daughter of James and Ann Long (late Whincup) born
                July 12, priv. bapt.

1809.	July 16.	Susannah daughter of James and Ann Aldis (late Chapman) born July 2, priv. bapt.
	Oct. 25.	Anna Maria daughter of Thomas and Elizabeth Lines (late Peake) born Sep. 2, priv. bapt.
1810.	March 18.	Thomas son of Nicholas and Mildred Buckingham (late Mabson) born Feb. 13
	April 15.	William son of James and Ann Mills (late Knight) born April 10, priv. bapt.
1809.	Jan. 31.	William son of Thomas and Margaret Walker (late Peak) born Feb. 15, 1806, priv. bapt.
1810.	Sep. 23.	William son of James and Ann Aldis (late Chapman) born Aug. 27
	May 20.	Robert son of Robert and Sarah Edments (late Reynolds) born May 17, privately. Received in the Church June 17
	July 22.	John son of James and Ann Finch (late Wickerton) born June 23
	July 15.	Jonathan Jeremiah son of Jonathan and Sarah Webb (late Dale) born July 9, priv. bapt.
1811.	April 12.	Maria daughter of William and Ann Shede (late Horn) born April 2, priv. bapt.
	Sep. 1.	Susan daughter of David and Mary Spall (late Baldry) born Aug. 25, priv. bapt.
1812.	Feb. 16.	Sophy daughter of Jeremia and Ann Broom (late Bulward) born Jan. 2
	April 5.	John son of Thomas and Elizabeth Lines (late Peake) born April 3, priv. bapt.
1811.	Nov. 17.	Charlotte daughter of James and Ann Aldis (late Chapman) born Oct. 25, pub. bapt. Nov. 17, 1811
1812.	June 28.	James son of Robert and Sarah Edments (late Reynolds) born June 25, priv. bapt.
	Aug. 16.	Sarah daughter of Benjamin and Mary Finch (late Scratton) born March 4
	Oct. 23.	Mary Anne daughter of James and Ann Aldis (late Chapman) Oct. 11, priv. bapt.
	Nov. 8.	James son of James and Ann Mills (late Knights) born April 26

Here end the Baptisms in the Second Volume.

1813.	March 21.	Mary Ann B.B. of Phillis Cross servant-maid by John Hamilton of Blythburg, labourer
	April 11.	Mary Ann daughter of William Shade, Laborer, and Ann (late Horn)
	May 30.	Timothy son of Thomas Smith, gardener, and Sarah (late Nestling)
	Nov. 14.	Harriet daughter of Simon Aldred, laborer, and Eliza (late Cross)

G

1814.	Jan. 3.	Henry Bence son of William Jones, Esq., and Matilda (late Bence) born Dec. 31, 1813. [*Afterwards the distinguished Dr Bence Jones*]
	Feb. 20.	Ann daughter of James Aldis, farmer, and Ann (late Chapman spinster)
	Feb. 27.	Maria daughter of William Wright, labourer, and Elizabeth born June 15, 1813
	April 24.	Benjamin son of Benjamin Finch, labourer, and Mary
	June 5.	Hepsiba daughter of Robert Turner of Blythburg, labourer, and Millison
	July 10.	Marianne daughter of William Benyfield, labourer, and Sarah
	Oct. 2.	Sarah daughter of Robert Edmunds, farmer, and Sarah. *On the margin*, Sarah Edments late Sarah Raynolds spinster
	Dec. 11.	John son of James Mills, labourer, and Anne
	Dec. 18.	Joseph William son of Joseph Sheppard, servant, and Mary
1815.	Jan. 8.	Martha daughter of James Aldis, farmer, and Ann (late Chapman spinster)
	Feb. 12.	Anne daughter of William Colthrop, labourer, and Elizabeth
	Feb. 12.	William son of Thomas Burgess, farmer, and Mary
	Aug. 20.	Harriett daughter of Joseph Spall, labourer, and Mary
	Oct. 29.	Emily Charlotte daughter of Thomas Limes,* farmer, and Elizabeth (late Peake)
	Dec. 3.	Marianne (base born) daughter of Philip Strowger, farmer, and Susan Fisher
1816.	Jan. 7.	Easter daughter of James Woodgate, labourer, and Sarah.
	April 7.	Ann daughter of James Aldis, farmer, and Ann (late Chapman spinster)
	May 16.	Henry Alexander Starkie (born May 15) son of Henry Bence Bence, Esq., and Elizabeth Susannah (late Starkie). [*Died at Thorington Hall, May 30, 1881*]
	Oct. 20.	Susan daughter of William Beddingfield, labourer, and Sarah (late Girling spinster)
1817.	Jan. 30.	Samuel (born Nov. 1, 1816) son of Robert Edments, farmer, and Sarah (late S. Raynolds)
	March 16.	William son of William Haylock, labourer, and Tabitha (late Morphew spinster)
	June 8.	Martha daughter of James Mills, labourer, and Ann (late Knights spinster)
	Aug. 17.	Elizabeth Ann (born Jan. 12) daughter of Thomas Burgess, farmer, and Mary Ann (late Lines spinster)
	Aug. 17.	William (born Feb. 6, 1815) son of Thomas Burgess, farmer, and Mary Ann (late Lines)
1818.	May 10.	Elizabeth daughter of William Haylock, labourer, and Tabitha (late Morphew spinster)
	May 24.	John (born Nov. 9, 1817) son of James Aldis, farmer, and Ann (late Chapman spinster)

* *Clerical error for Lines: see* 1809, 1812.

1818.	June 7.	Charles John (born Dec. 18, 1812) son of Charles Collier, clerk, and Kezia (late Baker daughter of John and Sarah Baker Dagenham, Essex. Buried at Walberswick)
	June 7.	Robert (born May 27, 1814) son of Nicholas Buckingham, farmer, and Mildred
	June 7.	Mary Ann (born Nov. 18, 1815) illegitimate daughter of Philip Strowger and Susan Fisher, servants
1819.	April 9.	Good Friday. John Goddard son of William Wright, labourer, and Elizabeth (died in infancy)
	June 13.	Eliza (born May 17) daughter of James Aldis, farmer, and Ann (late Chapman spinster)
	Oct. 24.	Thomas (born Wednesday, Sep. 15) son of Thomas Burgess, farmer, and Mary Ann (late Lines spinster)
	Nov. 21.	Elizabeth Mary (born Monday, April 4, 1814) daughter of Charles Collier, clerk, and Kezia (late Baker, K. B. spinster bapᵈ at Dagenham, Essex. Buried at Walberswick)
1820.	May 26.	Richard (born Friday, May 19) privately (recᵈ into the Church June 18) son of Samuel Edwards, labourer, ond Sarah (late Woodgate daughter of Rᵈ and Rᵗ Woodgate)
	June 4.	James (born Sat. June 5, 1819) illegitimate son of James Haylock, labourer, and Elizabeth Smith spinster
	June 18.	Robert son of James Woodgate, labourer, and Sarah (late Driver spinster)
	June 18.	Charlotte (born Thurs. April 6) daughter of James Woodgate, labourer, and Sarah (late Driver spinster)
	June 18.	Robert (born Tues. Feb. 16, 1819) illegitimate son of Sarah Lines spinster
	Oct. 23.	Samuel (born Tues. Oct. 10) son of James Mills, labourer, and Anne (late Knights spinster). (Recᵈ Nov. 12)
	Dec. 24.	Caroline (born Sunday, Nov. 26) 8ᵗʰ daughter now living and 11ᵗʰ child of James Aldis, farmer, and Ann (late Chapman)*
1821.	Jan. 6.	Louisa (born Friday, Dec. 29, 1820) daughter of William Beddingfield, labourer, and Sarah (late Girling) (died in infancy)
	April 7.	Catherine and Betsy (born Saturday, April 7) joint daughters of Robert Appletons, carpenter and joiner, and Susan (late Gooch)
	Aug. 16.	Elizabeth (born Monday, Jan. 24, 1820) daughter of Robert Edments, farmer, and Sarah (late Raynolds spinster)
	Oct. 21.	William (born Tuesday, Oct. 16) son of David Mayhew, labourer, and Elizabeth (late Lines)
	Nov. 18.	James (born Nov. 8) son of William Whiting, farmer, and Ann (late Hullet) recᵈ into Church June 16, 1826
1822.	March 31.	Ann daughter of George Smith, carpenter, and Mary his wife (late Raven) privately

* See Burials. Seven members of this family, victims of fever, were buried between Dec. 15, 1837, and April 13, 1838.

1822. May 15.   James son of William Row, labourer, and Susan his wife (late
                  Fisher) privately

       June 16.   Matilda daughter of William Noy, labourer, and Lydia (late
                  Browne)

       Oct. 27.   Mary daughter of Robert Rawlinson, labourer, and Sarah (late
                  Lines)

1823. June 8.   Sarah daughter of James Mills, labourer, and Anne (late
                  Knights)

       Aug. 27.   Edward Robert Starkie (born Aug. 26) son of Henry Bence
                  Bence, Esquire, and Elizabeth Susanna (late Starkie)
                  privately [*now living at Kentwell Hall in the Parish of
                  Long Melford, Suffolk*]

1824. Feb. 15.   Elizabeth (born Feb. 28, 1819) daughter of David Mayhew,
                  labourer, and Elizabeth (late Lines)

       Feb. 15.   James son of David Mayhew, labourer, and Elizabeth (late
                  Lines)

       May 30.   Rachael daughter of William Whiting, farmer, and Ann (late
                  Huflet) rec^d into Church June 16, 1826

       July 25.   Marianne natural daughter of Marianne Spall, servant

       July 25.   Elizabeth daughter of Joseph Spall, labourer, and Mary (late
                  Baldry). N.B. This child's name appears to have been
                  omitted in the Register when baptized about 5 years ago

       Oct. 2.   Thomas Starkie (born Oct. 1) son of Henry Bence Bence,
                  Esquire, and Elizabeth Susannah (late Starkie) privately.
                  [*Rector of Thorington, 1849 ; buried, 1858*]

1825. Jan. 30.   Susan daughter of William Rowe, labourer, and Susan (late
                  Fisher)

       Feb. 27.   William son of William Noy, labourer, and Lydia (late Browne)

       March 6.   Richard son of Richard Girling, farmer, and Elizabeth (late
                  Aldrich)

1826. Jan. 18.   William son of William Whiting, farmer, and Ann (late Huflet)
                  rec^d into Church June 16, 1826

       Oct. 29.   George John son of George Smith, carpenter, and Mary (late
                  Raven)

       Dec. 31.   William son of William Row, labourer, and Susan (late Fisher)

1827. Jan. 21.   George son of Robert Rawlinson, labourer, and Sarah (late
                  Lines)

       May 27.   William son of William Noy, labourer, and Lydia (late Browne)

       June 24.   William (born Sep. 1, 1825) son of John Rouse, carpenter,
                  and Mary (late Pearson)

       June 24.   Eliza (born Jan. 9) daughter of John Rouse, carpenter, and
                  Mary (late Pearson)

       Sep. 30.   William son of Charles Howard, labourer, and Sarah (late
                  Bayley)

       Nov. 24.   Daniel son of James Mills, labourer, and Ann (late Knights)

1828. Jan. 6.   Mary Girling daughter of Thomas Jacman, farmer, and Mary
                  (late Girling), privately, dead, *not buried in Thorington*

1828.	April 13.	James Henry son of James Friend, farmer, and Mary (late Rix) Rec⁴ into Church Dec. 25, 1828
	June 22.	Ann daughter of Samuel Philpot, labourer, and Phyllis (late Finch)
	Sep. 20.	James son of James Newson, labourer, and Sophia (late Shimming)
1829.	Jan. 4.	Sarah daughter of William Row, Lab', and Susan (late S. Fisher)
	Jan. 11.	Robert Mayhew son of William Whiting, farmer, and Ann (late Hufflet)
	April 19.	Matilda daughter of John Rouse, carpenter, and Mary (late Pearson)
	June 7.	Isaac son of William Noy, labourer, and Lydia (late Browne)
	July 19.	William Thomas son of George Smith, carpenter, and Mary (late Raven)
	Aug. 2.	Ann daughter of Robert Rawlinson, labourer, and Sarah (late Lines)
	Dec. 6.	Lina daughter of James Finch, labourer, and Susan (late Susan Watling)
1830.	May 9.	Frederic Samuel son of James Friend, farmer, and Mary (late M. Raikes)
	May 30.	Robert James son of James Peak, farmer, and Hannah (late H. Harvey)
	June 20.	George son of Robert Rawlinson, labourer, and Sarah (late S. Lines)
	July 11.	Emma daughter of John Rouse, carpenter, and Mary (late M. Peirson)
1831.	Feb. 13.	Samuel William son of Samuel Cross, farmer, and Mary (late M. Kersey)
	April 1.	Rachel daughter of James Newson, labourer, and Sophia (late S. Shimming)
	April 29.	Lucy daughter of William Row, labourer, and Susan (late S. Fisher)
	Aug. 28.	Mary Charlotte daughter of Daniel Hart, farmer, and Charlotte (late C. Aldis)
1832.	June 3.	William Chester son of James Friend, farmer, and Mary (late M. Raikes)
	Aug. 5.	Chester son of George Smith, carpenter, and Mary (late M. Raven)
	May 13.	John son of John Saker, labourer, and Mary (late M. Walker)
	Sep. 30.	Emily Ann daughter of Daniel Hart, farmer, and Charlotte (late Ch. Aldis)
	Oct. 7.	Emma daughter of Robert Rawlinson, labourer, and Sarah (late S. Lines)
	Oct. 21.	Eliza daughter of James Finch, labourer, and Susan (late S. Watling)

1832. Dec. 23. George Kersey son of Samuel Cross, farmer, and Mary (late M. Kersey)

1833. Feb. 24. Maria daughter of John Rouse, carpenter, and Mary (late M. Pearson)

March 3. Pamela daughter of William Lambert, thatcher, and Phœbe (late P. Calver)

May 19. John son of William Row, labourer, and Susan (late S. Fisher)

1834. April 6. Marianne daughter of James Friend, farmer, and Mary (late M. Rix)

April 27. Charlotte natural daughter of Amy Aldis, servant

June 22. Daniel Aldis son of Daniel Hart, farmer, and Charlotte (late Ch. Aldis)

1835. Feb. 1. Charlotte daughter of Robert Rawlinson, labourer, and Sarah (late S. Lines)

March 8. James son of Daniel Hart, farmer, and Charlotte (late C. Aldis)

April 19. English son of James Aldred, labourer, and Sarah (late S. Shade)

May 24. John son of William Haylock, labourer, and Tabitha (late T. Morphew)

Oct. 19. Harvey son of James Peak, farmer, and Hannah (late H. Harvey)

1836. March 6. George son of William Lambert, thatcher, and Phœbe (late P. Calver)

Sep. 18. John Edwin son of Daniel Hart, farmer, and Charlotte (late C. Aldis)

Oct. 16. Benjamin son of James Finch, labourer, and Susan (late S. Watling)

1837. May 14. Emily daughter of Robert Rawlinson, labourer, and Sarah (late S. Lines)

July 9. Charlotte daughter of William Row, labourer, and Susan (late S. Fisher)

Oct. 29. Samuel (born July 1834) son of John Saker, labourer, and Mary (late M. Walker)

1838. Nov. 11. John son of James Finch, labourer, and Susan (late S. Watling)

Dec. 2. Charles son of James Rush, farmer, and Sarah (late S. Etheridge)

1839. May 12. Betsy Sarah daughter of James Friend, farmer, and Mary (late M. Rix) received into Church Oct. 9, '53

1840. Jan. 19. Marianne daughter of John Saker, labourer, and Mary (late M. Walker)

Sep. 20. Sarah daughter of James Finch, labourer, and Susan (late S. Watling)

Nov. 15. James Harvey son of James Peake, farmer, and Hannah (late H. Harvey)

1841. April 11. Rebecca daughter of James Rush, farmer, and Sarah (late S. Etheridge)

1841.	April 11.	James son of James Rush, farmer, and Sarah (late S. Etheridge)
	Sep. 26.	Robert son of James Edments, farmer, and Ann (late A. Lyon)
1843.	Feb. 12.	Catherine daughter of James Rush, farmer, and Sarah (late S. Etheridge)
	Feb. 12.	Noah, son of John Mills, labourer, and Susaunah (late S. Rolleston)
	July 23.	Ann Maria daughter of James Finch, labourer, and Susan (late S. Watling)
	Sep. 10.	Harvey son of James Edments, farmer, and Ann (late A. Lyon)
1844.	May 5.	William son of William Catling, farmer, and Martha (late M. Matthews)
	Nov. 10.	Sarah daughter of James Rush, farmer, and Sarah (late S. Etheridge)
1845.	Jan. 5.	Sarah Ann daughter of James Edments, farmer, and Ann (late A. Lyon)
	July 6.	Henry son of William Roberts of Hinton, labourer, and Mary (late M. Howlett)
	July 27.	William son of James Finch, labourer, and Susan (late S. Watling)
	Dec. 14.	Elizabeth daughter of James Rush, farmer, and Sarah (late S. Etheridge)
1846.	April 26.	Emily daughter of James Edments, farmer, and Ann (late A. Lyon)
	Sep. 2.	Frederic son of William Catling, farmer, and Martha (late M. Matthews) (born Jan. 4)
1847.	July 25.	Robert (born Dec. 28, 1842) son of John Saker, labourer, and Mary (late M. Walker)
	July 25.	Rachel (born Dec. 8, 1844) daughter of John Saker, labourer, and Mary (late M. Walker)
	July 25.	Emma (born July 20, 1846) daughter of John Saker, labourer, and Mary (late M. Walker)

The three Sakers baptized July 25, 1847, were reported to me by their parents to have been born at the different times annexed to their respective names.

S. M. W.

	Nov. 14.	Emma (born Oct. 16) daughter of James Rush, farmer, and Sarah (late S. Etheridge)
1849.	June 17.	Edward son of William Roberts of Hinton, labourer, and Mary (late M. Howlett)
	Aug. 4.	Samuel Turner son of William Catling, farmer, and Martha (late M. Matthews)
1850.	Jan. 2.	Betsey, daughter of William Catling, farmer, and Martha (late M. Matthews)
	March 29.	William son of James Rush, farmer, and Sarah (late S. Etheridge)

1851.	Dec. 7.	Alice (born May 7) daughter of James Rush, farmer, and Sarah (late S. Etheridge)
1853.	Nov. 13.	Martha Maria daughter of Charles Gardiner Cobon, farmer, and Maria Arabella (late Legge)
	Dec. 1.	Agnes Marian daughter of Henry Alexander Starkie Bence Esq. and Agnes (late Barclay). Privately baptized at Portobello, Edinbro, by me T. S. Bence. Registered by Session Clerk, Duddingstone, Edinbro. [*Married July 6, 1876, to Percy Trower, Esq., at St. James', Piccadilly*]
1854.	June 20.	Sarah illegitimate daughter of William Tuthill and Emma Rawlinson
	Oct. 1.	John son of James Rush, farmer, and Sarah (late Etheridge)
	Oct. 8.	Margaret (born March 1, 1851) daughter of William Roberts of Hinton, labourer, and Mary (late M. Howlett)
	Oct. 8.	Samuel (born Dec. 1, 1852) son of William Roberts of Hinton, labourer, and Mary (late M. Howlett)
	Dec. 7.	George (born Oct. 14) son of Charles Gardiner Cobon, farmer, and Maria Arabella (late Legge)
1856.	Nov. 23.	Harry Charles son of William Catling, farmer, and Martha (late Matthews)
1858.	June 14.	Alfred William son of Henry Owles, farmer, and Susanna Maria
1859.	May 22.	William son of Daniel Mills, labourer, and Susan
	June 12.	John son of John Little, gamekeeper, and Mary Anne
	June 26.	Henry Edmund son of Samuel Betts Catlin, farmer, and Emily
	June 26.	Alice Louisa daughter of Samuel Betts Catlin, farmer, and Emily
	July 20.	Emma Mary daughter of Henry Owles, farmer, and Susannah Maria
1860.	Sep. 9.	Mary Jane daughter of James Thomas Mingay, farmer, and Jane (late Gray)
	Sep. 16.	Eleanor daughter of Henry Drew, butler, and Eleanor
	Sep. 28.	Edgar Frederick son of Henry Owles, farmer, and Susannah Maria
1861.	May 5.	Daniel son of Daniel Mills, labourer, and Susan
	Sep. 22.	Edgar William son of William Nunn, carpenter, and Emma
	Sep. 29.	Susan Elizabeth illegitimate daughter of Lucy Rowe, domestic
	Oct. 20.	Ida Agnes daughter of Henry Owles, farmer, and Susannah Maria
	Dec. 22.	Louisa daughter of George Gibbs, groom, and Mary
1862.	April 6.	Edward Groom, son of James Thomas Mingay, farmer, and Jane
1863.	Jan. 25.	George Addison (registered in the name of " Addison " only) son of Addison Bramwell, Clerk in Holy Orders, and Alice Fanny
	March 5.	William son of William Baldry, laborer, and Sophia
	March 15.	Elizabeth daughter of George Gibbs, groom, and Mary
	March 15.	Susan daughter of Daniel Mills, laborer, and Susan

1863.	May 17.	George son of William Crofford, labourer, and Sarah Anne
	May 17.	Emma daughter of the same
	May 17.	John son of the same
	May 17.	Charles son of the same
	Nov. 29.	Hannah daughter of Edward Bird, laborer, and Charlotte
1864.	Aug. 23.	George son of George Knights, laborer, and Mary Anne
1865.	Feb. 26.	Harriet Anne daughter of Daniel Mills, laborer, and Susan
	April 2.	Rosalie daughter of Henry Nesling, carpenter, and Lucilla Helen
	April 2.	Evelyn Gertrude daughter of the same
	May 7.	Alice Mary daughter of Addison Bramwell, Clerk in Holy Orders, and Alice Fanny
	June 4.	Alice daughter of Josiah Flatt, laborer, and Emma
	Nov. 19.	Jemima daughter of Edward Bird, laborer, and Charlotte
1866.	April 1.	Mary Anna daughter of George Knights, labourer, and Mary Anne
1867.	Feb. 24.	Edith daughter of Josiah Flatt, laborer, and Emma
	April 7.	Amy daughter of Addison Bramwell, Clerk in Holy Orders, and Alice Fanny [*buried Nov. 2, 1870*]
	Aug. 11.	Samuel daughter of Daniel Mills, laborer, and Susan
1868.	April 12.	Thomas son of Edward Bird, laborer, and Charlotte
	May 3.	Anna daughter of George Mayhew, laborer, ("no where house") and Rachel. [*"Nowhere House" is a cottage built on a small triangular piece of ground between Thorington and Wenhaston on the road to Blyburgh Common. It was formerly extra-parochial, but in 1862 was attached to Thorington.*]
	July 19.	Ellen daughter of George Knights, laborer, and Mary Anne
	Dec. 20.	Josiah son of Josiah Flatt, laborer, and Emma
1869.	Sep. 19.	Beatrice daughter of Addison Bramwell, Clerk in Holy Orders, and Alice Fanny
	Nov. 7.	Rosalie Matilda daughter of William Nunn, carpenter, and Emma
1870.	Jan. 9.	George son of Edward Bird, laborer, and Charlotte
1871.	March 5.	Edward Henry son of Henry Lane of Wenhaston, coachman, and Lucy
	May 21.	William son of William Baldry, laborer, and Sophia
	July 30.	John son of John Fenn, gamekeeper, and Susan
1872.	April 6.	Henry William (born April 3) son of William Belcher, Clerk in Holy Orders, and Edith Charlotte Musgrave [*buried the same day*]
	April 14.	William Rouse (born Aug. 26, 1871) son of William Nunn, carpenter, and Emma
	Sep. 15.	Robert Charles (born Aug. 15) son of Robert Taylor, laborer, and Charlotte
1873.	April 6.	Edward (born May 21, 1871) son of George Mayhew, laborer, and Rachel

1873.	April 6.	Margaret (born Jan. 31) daughter of George Mayhew, laborer, and Rachel
	April 6.	Charlotte (born March 5) daughter of Edward Bird, laborer, and Charlotte
	June 22.	William (born May 22) son of John Fenn, gamekeeper, and Susan
	Nov. 5.	Eva Maud (born Nov. 3) daughter of William Stammers Ray, farmer, and Mary Ann Judith
	Nov. 30.	Ernest John (born July 6) son of William Nunn, carpenter, and Emma
1874.	Jan. 25.	Edward (born Oct. 10, 1873) son of William Baldry, laborer, and Sophia
	Feb. 18.	Arthur (born Jan. 20) illegitimate son of Eliza Flatt, domestic servant
	May 3.	Edward James (born March 26) son of James Ablett, mariner, and Louisa
	Aug. 9.	Jane (born July 8) daughter of Robert Taylor, laborer, and Charlotte
	Aug. 27.	John William son of David Pearse, laborer, and Elizabeth Margaret
	Sep. 20.	Florence Eva (born Aug. 26) daughter of Edgar Catchpole, horseman, and Julia
	Nov. 1.	Adeline (born Sep. 12) daughter of William Clements of Eye, railway porter, and Margaret Roberts, singlewoman
1875.	Jan. 10.	William (born Nov. 16, 1874) son of John Fenn, gamekeeper, and Susan
	Jan. 24.	James (born Dec. 20, 1874) son of John Newson, laborer, and Caroline
	March 14.	John (born Feb. 7) son of Edward Bird of Wenhaston, laborer, and Charlotte
	July 4.	Mildred Eliza (born Sep. 30, 1874) daughter of George Beamish of Little Hulton, Lancashire, labourer, and Eliza
	Dec. 17.	Jane (born Nov. 23) daughter of Archer Hurren, gardener, and Alice
	Dec. 26.	Ursula (born Nov. 27) daughter of John Newson of Wenhaston, laborer, and Caroline
1876.	July 9.	William (born June 9) son of John Haylock, laborer, and Harriet (late Canham)
	Dec. 3.	Neailly (born Nov. 1) son of John Fenn, gamekeeper, and Susan (late Haylock)
	Dec. 3.	William (born Oct. 30) son of Archer Hurren, gardener, and Alice
1877.	Feb. 4.	Alice Maria (born Nov. 22, 1876) daughter of Edgar Catchpole, labouring man, and Julia
	March 4.	Henry (born Aug. 2, 1876) son of Robert Taylor, labouring man, and Charlotte (late Flatt)
	March 4.	Eliza (born Jan. 30) daughter of John Newson of Wenhaston, labouring man, and Caroline (late Eade)

1877.	May 27.	Henry Percy (born April 24) son of Percy Bence-Trower, Esq., of 7 Stanhope S^t, Hyde Park Gardens, London, and Agnes Marian (late Bence)
	Oct. 14.	Ursula Mary (born Sep. 17) daughter of Robert Smith of Wenhaston, groom, and Lucy (late Newson)
1878.	March 10.	Walter Edward (born Oct. 7, 1877) son of Emily Howard, daughter of the Sexton
	April 1.	Tabitha (born same day) daughter of John Haylock, labouring man, and Harriet (late Canham)
	April 14.	Emma (born Feb. 28) daughter of Robert Taylor, labouring man, and Charlotte (late Flatt)
	Sep. 22.	Agnes Helen (born Aug. 8) daughter of Percy Bence-Trower, Esq., of 7 Stanhope S^t, Hyde Park Gardens, London, and Agnes Marian (late Bence)
	Nov. 24.	Robert (born Oct. 26) son of John Fenn, gamekeeper, and Susan (late Haylock)
	Nov. 24.	George William (born Oct. 20) son of Edgar Catchpole, labouring man, and Julia (late Miles)
1879.	April 13.	Easter Day. Margaret (born June 10, 1877) daughter of George Mayhew, labouring man, and Rachel (late Roberts)
	April 13.	Easter Day. James (born Feb. 12) son of the same
	April 13.	Easter Day. Naomi Winifred (born Feb. 17) daughter of Charles Self of Wenhaston, labouring man, and Anna Maria (late Nolloth)
	Nov. 2.	Clementina (born Oct. 3) daughter of John Newson of Wenhaston, labouring man, and Caroline (late Eade)
	Dec. 28.	Charles Albert (born Nov. 5) son of Albert Haward of Wangford, bricklayer, and Elizabeth (late Eade)
1880.	Jan. 4.	Harriet Ann (born Nov. 17, 1879) daughter of George Mills, labouring man, and Jane (late Flatt)
	March 28.	Easter Day. Mary (born Feb. 1) daughter of John Haylock, labourer, and Harriet (late Canham)
	May 23.	Trinity Sunday. Annie Lucy (born April 21) daughter of Edgar Catchpole, labouring man, and Julia (late Miles)
	Sep. 26.	Alfred (born Aug. 10) son of Percy Bence-Trower, Esq., of 7 Stanhope S^t, Hyde Park Gardens, London, and Agnes Marian (late Bence)
	Oct. 31.	Kerenhappuck (born Sep. 29) daughter of John Fenn, gamekeeper, and Susan (late Haylock)
	Dec. 26.	Maud Mary (born Oct. 9) daughter of Arthur George Sarbutt of Lound, wheelwright, and Mary Ann (late Gibbs)
1881.	March 6.	Louisa (born Jan. 23) daughter of George Elmy of Hinton, labourer, and Emma (late Tombling)
	Sep. 25.	Louis George (born Apr. 20) son of Charles Self of Wenhaston, labouring man, and Anna Maria (late Nolloth)
	Sep. 25.	Elizabeth (born Aug. 9) daughter of Alfred Catchpole, horseman, and Elizabeth (late Gibbs)

MARRIAGES.

1594.		nulla
1595.	Sep. 2.	Edwarde Booth Gent. and Alice Pye
	Sep. 16.	John Stevnsone and Elizabeth Golde [*Robert Golde was Rector*]
	Sep. 29.	Thomas Turner and Margret Becket
	Oct. 1.	Thomas Johnson and Elizabeth Dryver
1596.	May 23.	Anthony Donnet and Marye Girlinge
	Sep. 5.	Thomas Gooch and Vasthye Corday
	Nov. 8.	John Wiseman and Elizabeth Watteline
1597.	Oct. 9.	William Sansame and Annys Rawlinge
	Oct. 17.	Edwarde Syer and Jane his wife
	Feb. 27.	Richarde Bartelet and Elizabeth Barker
1598.	Sep. 26.	Richard Spaldinge and Katharine Peacocke
	Oct. 1.	Richard Bennet and Margret Barnes
1599.	May 15.	Thomas Nuttall and Martha Laughter
1600.	Sep. 3.	John Crispe and Anne Toplife
	Feb. 23.	Thomas Crispe and Margery feveryeare
1601.	July 29.	John Broome and Marie Crispe
	Oct. 4.	William Cudden and Alice Barnes
1602—1606.		nulla
1607.	Feb. 8.	Thomas Floxe and Elizabeth Smyth
1608.	June 26.	Nicholas Kinge and Anne Aldinge
1609.	Feb. 12.	Thomas Trenchfeld widdower and Christian Smyth singlewoman
1610.		nulla
1611.	March 27.	Rob'te Baker widdower and Bridget Golde widdowe [*Mr. Paule Golde was buried 30 Sep. 1610, and Robert Golde was Rector 1593-1609 and 1612-1620*]
1613.	April 5.	Jaffery Haffen singleman and Mary Lewes singlewoman
	Sep. 23.	Thomas Osborne and Katharine Stiles
1614.	July 3.	William Markon and Elizabeth West
1615.	Nov. 3.	Henry Todde widdower and Abry Crispe widdowe
1616.	Oct. 20.	John Morley widdower and Joane Styles singlewoman
	Oct. 28.	Thomas Mickleborow singleman and Susan Peacocke singlewoman
1617.	Sep. 25.	Adam Norice and Margret Berry
	Nov. 20.	Augustine Bends singleman and Christian Vincent singlewoman
	Nov. 27.	Robt Reve and Alice Neave
1618.	Jan. 28.	John Ellet widdower and Anne Candler widdowe
	Feb. 9.	John Blythe and Anne Johnsone
1619—1621.		nulla
1622.	Sep. 19.	Rodulphus Rabbit* and Elizabeth Page
	Sep. 19.	Reginaldus French and Ann Rabbet*

* *See note Rabett family, p. 28.*

1622.	[—]	Thomas Beast and [blank] Andrewes widdowe
	Dec. 2.	Thomas Waters and Ellen Harvye widdowe
1623.	Oct. 15.	James Cleffard and Mathew* Rikard
	Oct. 20.	Timothy Haytbord and Grace Gerrand
	Oct. 23.	Robert fellow and Els Neusone
1624.	May 3.	Thomas Aldered and Mary Chikring
1625.	Sep. 22.	William Collet and Elizabeth Turner
1628.	Feb. 16.	Samuel Garroulde and Margaret Tirrold
	Feb. 16.	James Preston and Elizabeth Rogers
1629.	April 15.	James Clyforde and Anne Seevenpence†
	Oct. 1.	Thomas Joyner and Marye Greene
	Oct. 14.	John Scutt and Marye Houett
	Feb. 7.	Edward Scoulding and Alice Lessye
1630.	June 29.	Nicholas Ramsbye and Grace Jesoppe
	Oct. 5.	Roger Parker and Margaret Sepence
1631.	Nov. 5.	William Seppens and Marye Wesgate
1632.	Feb. 8.	John Keyrison and Susan Man
	March 3.	John Spalding yeoman and Margaret Thomazine widdowe
1635.	July 21.	Robert Leggate singleman and Rachel Gosling widdowe
1636.	Aug. 15.	John Cooke singleman and Sarah Mihils singlewoman
1637.	July 2.	Raynold Smyth and Susan Wilbye widdowe
	Oct. 27.	Robert Styles widdower and Sible Woods widdowe
	Sep. 28.	George Seppence singleman and Margaret Johnson singlewoman
	Sep. 26.	Richard Girling singleman and Alice Wincoppe singlewoman
1639.	Nov. 21.	John fliske and Marie Stan'ard
1640.	April 11.	John Reade and Katherine Chenye
	Sep. 27.	Edward Scoulding and Alice Barward
1641.	June 24.	Robt Sheapheard and Ann Marcon
	Oct. 7.	Ralph Tresswelle and Jane Miller
	Oct. 12.	John Smyth and Ann Thorne
	Jan. 6.	Willm Coan and Rose Asten
1654.	July 25.	Thomas Scote and ffrances forman wido
1655.	Oct. 14.	Robrt Bloweres and Grase Mordock wido
1657.	Dec. 3.	Richard Potter and Mary Pulham
1664.	Aug. 9.	ffrancis Bicraft and Susan Martin
1665.	Oct. 13.	Philip Patridge and Rebecca Evans [William Evans was Rector]
	April 26.	John Gotter and Anne Stimson
	May 11.	Joseph Hudson priest and Bathia Evan [William Evans was Rector]
	May 12.	Robert Savage and Anne Blobole
	Sep. 28.	John Sad and Anne Goodman
	Feb. 26.	William Crispe and Elizabeth Whiteing
1666.	April 17.	John Burcham and Sara Curtis
	May 1.	John Paul and Mary Eucrard

* Or Martha. See Burials, 1628, Jan. 14.
† See Marriages, 1623; and Burials, 1628.

1666.	Sep. 4.	Daniel Girling and Catherine Snelling
	Feb. 5.	Benjamin Crossby and Mary Fulgier
	Jan. 16.	Robert Cooke and Rose Cone
	Jan. 17.	Marke Clarke and Mary Herne
1667.	Sep. 5.	John Clarke of Eye and Margarett Pratt
	Sep. 19.	Edmund Watling and Margarett Sim'ons
	Sep. 25.	John Austin and Elizabeth Smith
	Nov. 14.	George Mosse and Catherine Nutle
	Jan. 14.	Francis Cooper and Elizabeth Rushmere
	Nov. 22.	Robert Downing and Frances Harman
	Jan. 23.	Marke Clarke and Han'a Mosse
	Feb. 4.	John Dalliman and Anne Clarke
	Feb. 11.	Stephen Rand and Mary Scouling
1668.	April 6.	Daniell Harper and Frances Lilly
	April [—]	Symon Astin and Mary Goodman
	Sep. 8.	Clement Gardner and Mary Smith
	Sep. 13.	Andrew King and Prudence Collison
1671.	May 30.	Robert Dymer and Annes Hubbard
	June 17.	John Poppie of Hoxen and Mary Caccamoate of Dickborough in Norfolk
	Aug. 1.	Willm Chapman and Mary Hadenham
	Nov. 6.	John Jeffery and Mary Blogatt
	Dec. 1.	Samuel Ludbrucke and Elizabeth Smith
	Dec. 10.	William Duffield and Mary Archer
1672.	April 23.	John Hane of Walberswicke and Lydia Cooper of Yoxford
	Sep. 11.	Willm Underwood of Laxfield and Jone Thrower of the same
	Sep. 27.	Willm Collett of Dunwich and Elizabeth Driver of the same
	Jan. 7.	Willm Nuson of Bramfield and Margarett Clarke of the same
	Jan. 7.	John Watling of Yoxford and Anne Noble of Weslton
1673.	April 1.	Nicholas Smith of Laxfield and Elen Moore of the same
	May 30.	Philip Fountaine of Halsworth and Jane Spindler of Whenhaston
	Sep. 18.	John Theoball and Anne Goddard of Huntingfield
	Oct. 18.	Thomas Browne of Walpole and Margaret Ellis of Bramfield
	Oct. 20.	Robert Boothe of Cookeley and Anne Patridge of Laxfield
	Oct. 21.	Robert Knights and Frances Browne of Halsworth
	Nov. 23.	John Hilling and Mary Grenacker of Dunwich
1674.	May 13.	Edward ffreeman of Spexhall and Han'ah Dreane of Midlton
	May 28.	Thomas Cocke of South Loppam in Norfolk and Susan Barrill of Huntingfield
	June 2.	James Turner of Rumburge and Elizabeth Baker of the same
	July 26.	Richard Creame of Laxfield and Margarett Cooke of the same
	July 26.	James Meeke of Wissett and Mary Spatchett of the same
	July 29.	Gabriel Barnes of Halsworth and Elizabeth ffurrow of Pakefield
	Aug. 13.	Francis Dokeing of Yoxford and Mary Copland of the same*

* At Yoxford—Mary Copland, d. of Will'm and Ann Copland baptised 6 Oct. 1649. Joannes Copland, M.B., died March 5, 1758. M.I. Rec. Daniel Copland, A.M., son of John and Mary

1674.	Oct. 5.	John Wade and Mercy Durrant
	Sep. 29.	Richard Aldrid and Elizabeth Ellis of Walpole
	Sep. 3.	Oliver Charburn* and Frances Gilder of Wesleton
	Nov. 2.	Edmund Gardner of Halsworth and Rebecca Taylor of Houlton
	Nov. 2.	John Cracknell of Tan'ingto' and Mary Fiske of the same
	Dec. 20.	Stephen Tunkes of Halsworth and Mary Welles of Blithburgh
	Dec. 26.	Thomas Hastinges of Feberto and Lettice Alexander of the same
	Dec. 27.	Gabriel Farrow of Pakefield and Brigett Seager of Halsworth
	Dec. 30.	Nicolas Greenaker of Dunwich and Susan Driver of Darsham
	Jan. 1.	Robert Tansley of Dunwich and Mary Nursie of the same
1675.	April 6.	Nicolas Giles [the G is written over the letter M] of Cookeley and Mathe Milles of the same
	April 6.	Henry Perse of Halsworth and Frances Spencer of Sotturton
	April 8.	John Steele of Alderburge and Mary Raynes of the same
	April 8.	John Harling of Huntingfield and Anne Nicolls of Wenhaston
	April 15.	Thomas Seager of Wenhaston and Susan Dunthorn of the same
	May 13.	Robert Patridge and Als Payne
	July 4.	Henry Ward and Mary Girling
	Aug. 12.	Luke Raydon of Alderburge and Margaret Tayler of Walpole
1677.	Dec. 16.	John Edwards and Mary Poole
	Feb. 17.	Henry Snowling and Hester Claxton
1678.	April 2.	Anthony Julians of Yoxford and Elizabeth Goodhall
	May 20.	James Drane of Middleton and Sarah Browne of ffordley
	Oct. 10.	William Mason of Southwold and Elizabeth Hall of the same
	Oct. 20.	Henery Lillie of Henham and Margret Girling of the same
	Oct. 21.	Benjamen Bayes† of Whesleton clerk and Priscilla Manning‡
1679.	June 11.	John Savage of Shaddingfield and Dorothy Dew of Henham
1695.	Feb. 24.	ffrancis Lilbourn of Yoxford and Susan Brown of this parish

Copl'wā, vicar of Yoxford for 40 years, instituted 1753. Patron, Sir John Rous, Bart. Died 29 March, 1793. M.I.

* The name Chathurne, or Charborne, occurs frequently in the Westleton Registers. Oliver Chathourne signs his name as vicar first in 1608. He was buried 30th May, 1627. There is a small square stone to his memory on the floor of the vestry to the east of the chancel in Westleton Church :—

OLIVER CHATBVRNE CLARKE WAS BVRIED THE 30 OF MAY 1627.

Margaret, d. of Oliver Chathourne, Clarke, bap. 25 Oct. 1609. Robert, bap. 13 Aug. 1612. Mary, bap. 23 March 1614; bur. 8 Sep. 1615. Oliver, bap. 6 July 1616.

Sarry, da. of Ollifer and Mary Charborne, bur. 2 June 1654.

Oliver, son of Oliver Chathurn and Francis his wife, bap. 3 Nov. 1675; bur. 7 Aug. 1677. Oliver, son of the same, bap. 30 March 1679.

Mrs. Mary Chathurn, bur. 12 Aug. 1683.

Oliver Chathurn of Walpole, bur. 15 May 1695.

† There is no record of the Rev. Benjamin Bayes in the Westleton Registers or Parish Papers.

‡ There is no further trace of Priscilla Manning's family in this parish. The name, however, prevailed in the neighbourhood. Some of them were Nonconforming ministers ejected in 1662, or afterwards. Of these were John Manning, of Peasenhall, died 1691; Samuel Manning, of Walpole, he was the first minister of the Dissenting interest at Walpole 1647; William Manning, of Middleton, died 1711 (Nonconformist Memorials. Suffolk, ii., 434, 435, 438).

1696.	Oct. 6.	William Wade of Westleton and Mary Strowger of Halesworth
	Nov. 8.	John Prudence singleman of Martham in Norfolk and Mary Clerke of Halesworth
1697.	April 15.	Thomas Dade and Mary Ward of Halesworth
	Nov. 7.	Thomas Wales* and Cecily Crisp of Halesworth
1698.	Dec. 29.	Edmund Anguish of Somerleighton Gent.† and Mary the

* *Many members of the family of Wales are buried in Walberswick Churchyard, and the following entry from the Halesworth Registers indicates a relationship between the Walberswick and Halesworth branches:—1751, June 28, Carver Wales, of Walderswick, merchant, burd. (The name Carver is probably derived from Thomas Carver, Doctor of Physick, who was buried at Halesworth 6th October 1708.) The name is now quite extinct at Walberswick. A branch of the family settled at Downham Market, and descendants are still living in that neighbourhood.*

† The following notice of the Anguish family is copied from Suckling's 'Suffolk,' vol. ii., pp. 44, 45 :—

"Thomas Garneys, Esq., in 1672, conveyed the whole village and manor of Somerleyton to Admiral Sir Thomas Allin, Knt. and Bart., who died in 1686. He left two children—Sir Thomas Allin, Bart., who succeeded him, but died without issue ; and Alice Allin, who, marrying Edmund Anguish. Esq., of Moulton, in Norfolk, carried Somerleyton and the adjoining estates into that family, their eldest son, Richard Anguish, taking the name and arms of Allin under the provisions of his uncle's will. Sir Richard Allin, *alias* Anguish, was advanced to the rank of a Baronet, and married, in 1699, Frances, daughter of Henry Ashurst. [Le Neve calls her Diana Ashurst.] He died about the year 1725, leaving two sons—Sir Thomas Allin, Bart., who succeeded him, but died unmarried ; and Ashurst Allin, who, on his brother's death, inherited his baronetcy and estates. Sir Ashurst married Thomasin Norris, and dying in 1770, devised his property to his only son, Sir Thomas Allin, who died in 1794, a bachelor ; in whose person this line of the family and the baronetcy became extinct. The manor of Somerleyton, however, and the residue of the estates, passed to his heir-at-law, Thomas Anguish, Esq., who was descended from Edmund Anguish, the second son of Edmund Anguish, Esq., of Moulton aforesaid, who married Alice, daughter of the first Sir Thomas Allin. Mr. Anguish died unmarried in 1810 (he was a lunatic in 1806, vol. i., p. 243), and was succeeded in all his manors by the Rev. George Anguish, Clerk, M.A., Prebendary of Norwich Cathedral (and Rector of Gisleham, vol. i., p. 249). This gentleman was born February 7th, 1764, and dying a bachelor July 5th, 1843, the family of Anguish became extinct. The manor and advowson of Somerleyton then fell by heirship to his nephew, Lord Sydney Godolphin Osborne, son of the Duke of Leeds, by Catharine, his second wife, sister to the Rev. George Anguish, the previous possessor. In August, 1844, these, with several other lordships and estates, were conveyed, [*by purchase*] as already shewn, to Samuel Morton Peto, Esq., [afterwards Sir S. M. Peto, Bart.,] of the City of London, who is the present possessor (1847). The family of Anguish, late lords of Somerleyton, are said to have migrated from the shire of Angus, in Scotland, whence they assumed their surname. Their crest, however, does not confirm this, being an anguis, or snake, coiled in the grass. The shield is a good old bearing : gules, a cinquefoil, pierced, argent. Blomefield says, 'They settled at Moulton, in Norfolk, where they remained three centuries, and where, in 1699, Edward Anguish held the manor of the Earl of Northampton, as parcel of the manor of Forcet.'"

The following properties were also held [Suckling's 'Suffolk.' vol. i.] by the Allins and Anguishes, and devolved on Lord S. G. Osborne, who sold them to Mr. Peto, August 1844. The lordship of the hundred of Mutford ; the lordship of the manor of Barnaby ; Carlton Colville (the advowson was sold for £3000 to W. Andrews, Esq.); the estates in Mutford, which Sir Thomas Allin had bought of the Trustees of Lady Mary Heveningham, wife of William Heveningham, who at the Restoration was attainted of high treason and his estates were confiscated for acting as one of the judges at the trial of Charles I. ; the fee of the hundred of Lothingland ; the manors of Ashby with the advowson of the church, and the manors of Corton and Newton, with the appurtenances and 4 messuages, 3 gardens, 50 acres of land, 20 of meadow, 40 of pasture, 10 of wood, 200 of furze and heath, 10 of marsh, 10 of alder, 40 shillings rent, and free-foldage in Ashby, Corton, Newton, Oulton, Lowestoft, and Hopton ; the manor and estates of Gapton Hall, wit

MARRIAGES. 57

daughter of Will'm Betts of Yoxford Gent. both single*

1698. Feb. 16. Robert Brown of this parish and Hannah Turner of Sibton both single

1699. Aug. 10. John Gardener and Priscilla Cuddon both single and of Halesworth

Nov. 9. Robert Lilly of Blyford widower and Ann Ashley of Henham singlewoman

Jan. 9. John Browne of this parish and Ann Battely of Rumberg both single

Jan. 11. Edward Browne of Cheston singleman and Mary Hugman of Halesworth singlewoman

Jan. 23. William Burward of Blyford widower and Catherine Browne of Yoxford singlewoman

1700. July 23. Charles Perry of Herringfleet Gent. and Eleanor Jenkenson of Cheston both single

Oct. 17. Richard Poller of Wisset widower and Philippa Canhop of Bramfield widow

Nov. 28. Henry Nursey of Halesworth singleman and Elizabeth Lee of Wesleton singlewoman

1700-1. Feb. 19. Robert Copping of Bramfield vid. and Mary Chapman of the same singlewoman

Feb. 27. Richard Keeble of Westhall singleman and Catherine Reeve of the same singlewoman

1700. Sep. 16. James Symons and Alatheia Rous of Darsham single persons

March 1. Nich. Ewen and Philippa Todd

1701. Oct. 9. John Abel of Mettingham singleman and Elizabeth Syal of Halesworth singlewoman

1702. Sep. 29. John Blowers and Hannah Burrard both single

Oct. 9. Richard Smith and Hannan Attershall single persons of Halesworth

1703. Sep. 30. John Bacon and Martha Rush

1704. April 27. John Pepper and Elizebeth Larter

June 8. John Collett of Halesworth singleman and Margerett Barfoot singlewoman

Belton ; the manors of Blundeston Hall and Gunville's [the Gunville's *estate* was sold by the executors of Frances, daughter of the Rev. Ashurst Allin, to Nicholas Henry Bacon, Esq.] (the advowson of Blundeston with Flixton Lord S. G. Osborne sold to Thos. Morse, Esq.); the manors of Somerleyton, Flixton, Corton, Ashby, Gapton, and Newton; the manor of Lawney in Flixton; the manors of East and West and North and South Leet in Gorleston, and of Gorleston. Sir S. M. Peto was head of the firm Peto, Betts, and Co., Contractors, who laid down the railway from Balaclava to Sebastopol during the Crimean war free of charge to the English Government beyond the cost price ; for this service he received a baronetcy. On the bankruptcy of the firm, 1866, the Somerleyton property was sold to Sir Francis Crossley, Bart., M.P. for the West Riding, Yorkshire. His son, Sir Savile Crossley, is the present possessor.

* *Mary, d. of William and Dorothy Betts, baptized 19 July 1676. William Betts, Attorney-at-Law, buried 3 March 1709. William Betts, Attorney-at-Law, buried 12 Dec. 1718. Dorothy Betts, widdow, was buried 20 July 1732 at Yoxford.*

I

1704.	July 24.	John Brook Gent. of Norwich and Rose Edwards of Halesworth widdow
	Sep. 29.	Will. Gale and Eliz. Singler
1707.	Oct. 18.	Tho. Jackson widdower and Mary Blowers singlewoman
1708-9.	March 24.	Tho. Clark singleman and Eliz. Ludbrook singlewoman
1711-12.	Jan. 7.	Joseph Julians of Peasenhall singleman and Susan Nolloth of this parish singlewoman
1712.	July 17.	John Saunders of Wenhaston widdower and Elizebeth Ewin of this parish widdow
1714.	Nov. 23.	William flisk of Peasenhall and Elizebeth Pattridge of Cratfield
1714-5.	Jan. 13.	John Julians of Easton and Mary Scott of Thorington
1720.	Sep. 22.	William Soanes of Halesworth and Sarah Gibbs of the same
1721.	Sep. 23.	William Harvey and Anne Coke
1722.	Oct. 30.	John Mollett of Darsham widdower and Susan Skoulding of the same singlewoman
1721.	Nov. 7.	Geo. Tunn widower and Anne Reeve both of Middleton
1723.	April 16.	William Lurrood of Bramfield widdower and Elizebeth Scott of Thorington singlewoman
1723-4.	Feb. 25.	Alexander Bloss and Elizebeth Field
1725.	April 8.	Joseph Lambert and Mary Caton both of Halesworth
	Sep. 28.	Benjamin Curtis and Mary Higgins both of Darsham
	Sep. 9.	Edmund Alden and Elizebeth Hartly widdow both of Halesworth, by License [first mention of License]
1726.	Dec. 1.	Alexander Bloss and Anne Lamb, by Banns [first mention of Banns]
1727.	June 15.	Everard Woods* of Westleton widdower and Sarah Osborn of the same singlewoman, by License by Mr Hudson
1728.	Dec. 3.	Henry Bull and Matthew Short both single
	Dec. 31.	Arthur Applewhait of Huntingfield and Bridgett Nelson of Bramfield, by License

* The family of Woods lived in Westleton for many generations. There are memorial slabs on the floor of the chancel, and tablets on its walls, to the following members:—

John Woods, gent., died 7 Oct. 1703, aged 57. Mary, his wife, daughter of James Knapp, of Wingfarthing, co. Norfolk, gent., died 19 Sept. 1720, aged 70.

Margaret, wife of Everard Woods, gent., died 8 March 1725, aged 31. Everard, their son, died 7 Sept. 1718, aged 6 months. Mary, their daughter, died 6 Jan. 1720, aged 1 month. Everard Woods, gent., died 1 May 1741, aged 50. Sarah, his second wife, died 9 May 1743, aged 46.

Mary, wife of John Woods, gentleman, died 15 Dec. 1736, aged 12. Three of their children who died in infancy—Mary, died 2 June 1714; Margaret, died 1 July 1720; Ann, died 1 April 1729. John Woods, gentleman, died 15 June 1718, aged 59.

William Woods, died 13 Aug. 1764, aged 46. Elizabeth Woods, his wife, died 22 July 1788, aged 69.

Sarah, wife of Alexander Woods, gent., died 13 Jan. 1783, aged 37.

Margaret, wife of Everard Woods, died 5 April 1781, aged 63.

John Woods, late of Halesworth, gent., died 15 March 1793, aged 63   Hannah, his wife, died 6 Nov. 1820, aged 86.

William Woods, gent., died 29 Nov. 1830, aged 47.

On the Chancel Floor of Bramfield Church are the following
Monumental Inscriptions :—

Here lies the Body of Arthur Applewhaite
Second Son of Henry Applewhaite
of Huntingfield in this County, Gent,
(who was Favourite and Bayliff to
Henry Heveningham, Henry Heron,
and John Bence, Deceased, and remains
so to Alexander Bence and George
Dashwood, All Esquires, and successively
owners of the Heveningham Hall Estate)
who died on the ninth day of September
A.D. 1733. And in the 39ᵗʰ year of his Age.

He married Bridgett the Eldest Daughter
And at length, Sole Heiress of Lambert
Nelson, late of this Parish, Gent, By whom
he had no Issue, and to whom (Having by
his Father's Instigation made no will)
He left no Legacy but a Chancery-
Suit with his Eldest Brother For her
own Paternal Estates in this Town
and Blyford.

M. S.

Between the Remains of her Brother Edward
and of her Husband Arthur
Here lies the Body of Bridgett Applewhaite
once Bridgett Nelson
After the Fatigues of a Married Life
Born by her with Incredible Patience
for Four Years and three Quarters, bating three weeks,
and after the Enjoiment of the Glorious Freedom
of an easy and Unblemisht Widowhood
For four years and upwards
She Resolved to run the Risk of a second Marriage Bed
But Death forbad the Banns—
and having with an Apoplectick Dart

John Woods, late of Darsham, died 26 Feb. 1839, aged 50. Sarah, his wife, died 28 March 1851,
aged 59. Their children—Harriet Rachel, died 21 Aug. 1842, aged 15 ; Mary, died 18 Feb. 1843,
aged 22 ; Sarah Elizabeth, died 25 March 1843, aged 25 ; Elizabeth Annie, died 25 June 1843,
aged 23 ; and seven died in infancy.
Susanna Maria, wife of Samuel Alexander Woods, died 6 May 1848, aged 71. Samuel Alex-
ander Woods, died 25 Oct. 1857, aged 75.
Samuel Alexander Woods, died 23 May 1863, aged 59. Rachel, his wife, died 8 Dec. 1838
aged 33. Maria Elizabeth, their daughter, died 29 Sept. 1859, aged 26.
The last of the family left the parish of Westleton about 1870.

(The same Instrument with which he had Formerly
Dispatcht her Mother)
Toucht the most vital part of her Brain ;
She must have fallen Directly to the Ground
(as one Thunderstrook)
If she had not been catcht and Supported
by her Intended Husband.
Of which Invisible Bruise
After a struggle for above sixty Hours
With that grand Enemy to Life
(But the certain and Mercifull Friend to Helpless Old Age)
In Terrible Convulsions Plaintive Groans or Stupefying Sleep
Without Recovery of her Speech or Senses
She dyed on the 12ᵗʰ day of Sepʳ in yᵉ year { of our Lord 1737
{ of her own age 44

1729.	May 26.	Samuell Meene of Sᵗ James South-Elmham widdower and Eliza-beth Fox of Rumboro, by a License from the Chancellour
	Nov. 4.	Thomas Fella* and Mary Rivett
	Dec. 2.	John French widdower and Elizebeth Gorin
1731.	Sep. 30.	Mark Blowers and Frances Turner
1732.	May 29.	Stephen Webster, woollen-draper, of Halesworth and Mary Howe's of Rumborow, by License
	June 12.	John Barber of Cratfield and Mary Goodwin of Rumborow by License
	Sep. 26.	Thomas Turpin of Westhall widower and Hannah Goodall widow of Thorington
1733.	Jan. 27.	Christopher Jarvis and Sarah Wallich
1737.	Sep. 26.	Richard Page of Yoxford and Susan Todd of Thorington
1739.	April 26.	John Solomon and Lydia Newman both single
	Nov. 1.	Nicholas Barber and Ann French of Rumburgh single persons
	Jan. 9.	George Spatchet wid. and Susan Harlock singlewoman both of Rumburgh
1741.	April 2.	Mʳ John Moore of Halesworth widower and Mʳˢ Catherine Butcher widow of Yoxford, by License. [Dennis Butcher and Catharine Elsden both single were married at Yoxford 28 Sep. 1728. Dennis Butcher married man was buried there 23 Sep. 1738, aged 32.]

* The Halesworth Registers abound with Fella entries. In the church chest there is a very interesting folio MS. in the handwriting of Thomas Fella, giving an account of the family of Launce. It is a remarkable specimen of caligraphy. The merchant's mark of the writer is repeated twice in the volume, a woodcut of which is here given.

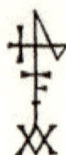

1742.	Sep. 14.	Thomas Bigsby of Woodbridge Hacheston and Elizabeth Tillett of Sibton both single
	Nov. 16.	Thomas Randal of Bramfield singleman and Elizabeth Wilson singlewoman of Walderswick, by License
1743.	Nov. 20.	Richard Nunn and Susannah Pallant both of Bramfield
1744.	June 22.	William Parish of Wenhaston widower and Sarah Pells of Thorington spinster
	July 2.	Francis Woolnough of Bramfield singleman and Elizabeth Kettle of the same singlewoman
	Oct. 1.	Edward Turpentine and Ann Smith
	Oct. 21.	Augustus Bedwell of Yoxford singleman and Martha Foulsham of Sibton singlewoman, by License
1744-5.	Jan. 31.	Thomas Wade and Sarah Losson both of Bramfield, by License
	Feb. 12.	William Utting and Mary Parsley both of Bramfield
1745.	Oct. 20.	John Denny and Sarah Clark both single persons of Halesworth, by License
	Oct. 29.	Richard Hurrin and Sarah Garwood both single
1746.	June 29.	William Nunn of Friston and Sarah Eastaugh of Bramfield, by License
	Oct. 16.	Samuel Edwards and Susannah Woolnough, by License
1746-7.	Feb. 17.	Edward Burwood and Mary Watling, by License
	March 3.	Richard Clark and Elizabeth Downing, by License
1747.	Oct. 26.	James Colthorp and Martha Godbold
1748.	Sep. 13.	Stephen Sanders of Peasenhall and Elizabeth Blowers of Sibton, by License
1749.	Aug. 9.	Daniel Partridge and Mary Wilson both single, by Mr Shipman
	Oct. 17.	George Lane and Elizabeth Scolding both of Walpole, the Banns being first duly publish'd at Walpole
1750.	April 16.	John Field of Walderswick and Elizabeth James, the Banns being first duly published at Walderswick and Thorington
	Aug. 29.	Nathaniel Briggs and Mary Newson both of Walpole
	Sep. 12.	William Hadingham of Heveningham and Margaret Elliot of Cransford
1751.	Aug. 7.	John Puttock and Sarah Cadey were married at Thorington, their Banns being first published at Bramfield (they belonging to that place)
	Oct. 1.	Thomas Baxter of Halesworth and Sarah Lambert of Blithburgh, by License
1752.		None
1753.*	March 2.	Ralph Baldry of Mendham and Hannah Giduey of Hinton, by License

* In 1753 an Act of Parliament which was to come into operation March 25, 1754, was passed to prevent clandestine marriages. Hitherto many persons had solemnized matrimony in prisons and other places without publication of banns or license, and it was now enacted that banns of marriage must be published on three separate Sundays preceding the marriage in the church or chapel of the parish wherein the persons to be married dwelt, or if they lived in different parishes then in the church or chapel of each parish in which they dwelt ; and the marriage was

1753. July 8.   Matthew Todd and Deborah Wilkinson both of Bramfield, by
                   License

      Aug. 27.   Samuel Cotton and Martha Jessup both of Blithburgh, the Banns
                   being first duly published at Blithburgh by Mʳ Copland

      Oct. 11.   The Revᵈ Barnabas Symonds Clerk of Kellishall and Elizabeth
                   Brown of Benhall, by License (see "*Rectors of Tho-
                   rington*," p. 9)

      Dec. 26.   Jeremiah Aldrich Jun. of Saxmundham and Mary Knights of
                   the same, the Banns being first published at Saxmundham
                   by the Revᵈ Mʳ Hill

1754, 55, 56, 57, 58. None

1759. March 5.   Samuel Harbor of Thorington and Mary Reeve of Wenhaston
                   both single, by License

to be solemnized in one of the churches or chapels where the banns had been published, and in
"no other place whatsoever." Power was reserved to the Bishops to grant licenses, and to the
Archbishop of Canterbury to grant special licenses. Any person convicted of solemnizing matrimony without banns or license or in any other place than the proper church or chapel, was to
"be transported to some of His Majesty's plantations in America for the space of fourteen years,"
and the marriage to be "null and void," but the prosecution must be commenced "within three
years after the offence committed." Marriage was to be solemnized in the presence of at least
two witnesses besides the minister. The penalty for making a false entry in the register book
"of any matter or thing relating to any marriage," or forging or altering an entry or the copy
of an entry. or forging or altering a license, or destroying any register book or any part of one,
with intent to void a marriage, was " death as a felon without benefit of clergy " (*The Statutes
at Large*, Pickering, vol. xxi., p. 124).

*Considering the widespread illegal publication of banns in use among the clergy the following
note may be of interest :—*

The rubric before " The Form of Solemnization of Matrimony " in "the Sealed Books " which
by the Act of Uniformity has the force of Statute Law, is as follows : " First, the banns of all
that are to be married together must be published in the church three several Sundays or holy-
days in the time of divine service, immediately before the sentences for the offertory." The
rubrics only provide for the publication of banns after the Nicene Creed. This was inconvenient
where there was not divine service in the morning of every Sunday. To remedy this, the
Marriage Act. 26 Geo. II., c. 33 (1753), orders the banns to be published " upon three Sundays
preceding the solemnization of matrimony, during the time of Morning Service, or of Evening
Service if there be no Morning Service, in such church or chapel upon any of those Sundays,
immediately after the second lesson." The words, " after the second lesson," are to be taken
with the alternative clause only ; the time of publication when there is a Morning Service being
already fixed by the rubric. There was no reason for changing the time of publication in the
Morning Service, the only thing needed being a permission to publish banns of marriage during
the Evening Service.

Note.—This is the legal opinion of Mr. A. J. Stephens (*Notes on the Book of Common Prayer*,
vol. ii., p. 1153): " The printers of the Prayer Book have committed a flagrant breach, or rather
a succession of flagrant breaches of the law ; for they have not only chosen to put their own
construction on the statute, which undoubtedly is a false one, but they have, in order to carry
out their false construction, actually omitted altogether that portion of the rubric after the
Nicene Creed which directs the publication of the banns, and also substituted a new rubric of
their own at the commencement of the marriage service, although the statute says nothing
which in the remotest degree authorizes any alteration of the rubric, but rather guards against
any unnecessary deviation from it " (Scudamore's *Notitia Eucharistica*, pp. 253-4). *The rubric
after the Nicene Creed in the Sealed Books is as follows, " And then also (if occasion be) shall
notice be given of the Communion ; and the banns of matrimony published," etc. The rubric
before the Marriage Service is given above.*

1760.	Oct. 9.	Henry Tillet of Bramfield and Frances Potter of Thorington both single
1775.	Oct. 3.	Thos Haward widr and Rach' Cullham single
1776.	Jan. 5.	John Ditcher of Darsham and Mary Aldiss, Thorington, singles
1783.	Jan. 23.	William Abbet and Sarah Coper both single
	Sep. 8. .	John Pepper of Halesworth widower and Hannah Briggs of Thorington singlewoman, by License

Here end the Marriages in the First Volume.

SECOND VOLUME OF MARRIAGES, 1754 TO 1812 INCLUSIVE.

On the inside of the cover is this memorandum :—

Nov. 1, 1806. The Rev. Bence Bence was inducted into this living by the Rev. Tho. Sheriffe, R. of Uggeshall, and he read himself in on the following day.

In this book witnesses for the first time attest their presence at the ceremony. In 1757 Charles Mahourn, Rector, performs the marriage service and also signs the Register as one of the two witnesses ; and in 1758, 1770, 1772, and 1773, Barnabas Symonds, Rector, does the same.

It will be noticed that all the entries in the first volume of Marriages after 1758 are repeated in this book, and that in this book entries of Marriages are made during the years 1754, 5, 6, 7, 8, whilst in the first book it is noted that in these same years there were " none."

1754.	Aug. 6.	William Woodyard and Mary Knights both single
1755.	May 8.	Thomas Freeman of Blythburgh and Elizabeth Docking of Thorington a minor with consent of parents, by License
1756.	Dec. 23.	Samuel Stronger and Ann Wickerton both single
1757.	Aug. 11.	Thomas Turner and Mary Copping of Bramfield both single
1758.	Feb. 20.	James Canham husbandman and Mary Rimmington both single
	May 30.	Robert Spore Junior and Margaret Rappett both single, by License
	Nov. 2.	John Tutthill and Amy Jerny both single
	Dec. 7.	Robert Spore widower and Alice Spall singlewoman
1759.	Feb. 22.	William Turner of Brandiston and Ann Copping both single
	March 5.	Sam' Harbar singleman and Mary Reeve of Wenhaston, by License
1760.	Feb. 11.	Sam' Graystone of Halesworth and Eliz. Baxter both single
	[—] 9.	Henry Tillet of Bramfield, mason, and Frances Porter both single
1761.	July 20.	James Tyrrell of Wenhaston and Mary Bickers both single
	Dec. 29.	Wm Goddard and Sarah Studd both single
1762.	Jan. 19.	George Golding Esq. of Poslingford and Ann Bence both single, by License [Ann Golding, bur. Oct. 31, 1794, M.I. George Golding, bur. Dec. 29, 1803].
	May 24.	Peter Wickerton and Ann Green both single
	Sep. 13.	William Spore and Mary Havers both single
	Oct. 19.	Samuel Elmy and Sarah Jarvis both single

1764. Oct. 9. Robert Hitcham widower and Mary Butcher singlewoman

1766. Aug. 22. William Bickers of Wenhaston widower and Elizabeth Samson singlewoman

1769. Jan. 5. Charles Green of Clare and Ann Blackwall both single [*Geo. Golding and Ann Golding are the two witnesses*]

Nov. 12. James Philpott and Rose Smith both single

1770. Nov. 12. Thomas Richardson and Sarah Burwood both single

1772. Feb. 10. Thomas Rendhall of Tunstall and Ann Aldiss both single

April 2. Cornelius Roberts and Elizabeth Nolloth both single

1773. Aug. 30. William Nolloth and Martha Buller both single

Oct. 14. Edward Catchpole of Wenhaston and Hannah Masterson both single

1775. Oct. 3. Thomas Haward widower and Rachael Cullum singlewoman

1776. Jan. 5. John Ditcher of Darsham and Mary Aldiss both single

1777. Oct. 23. William Crisp of Bramfield and Elizabeth Atkins both single, by License

1778. June 23. Robert Gillman of Bramfield and Sarah Savage both single

1779. Oct. 11. John Smyth and Mary Berry both single

1783. Jan. 23. William Abbet and Sarah Coper both single

Sep. 8. John Pepper of Halesworth widower and Hannah Briggs single woman, by License

1785. Sep. 29. Thomas Day and Elizabeth Studd both single

Nov. 11. William Haylock and Elizabeth Wickerton both single

Nov. 24. William Engall of Saxmundham singleman and Elizabeth Hall a minor with consent of parents, by License

1787. May 18. James Finch and Ann Wickerton both single

1788. Jan. 29. Philip Strowger and Mary Canham both single, by License

1789. Jan. 13. Jonathan Rackam of Benacre and Ann Goodwin both single

1790. March 15. Tall Clark and Mary Cable of Bramfield both single

Sep. 14. Elijah Phillippoe of Wenhaston widower and Lisabel Woodgate singlewoman

1791. May 20. Thomas Walker and Margaret Peake both single, by License

1792. May 9. Thomas Lines of Thorpe Parva in Norfolk and Elizabeth Peak both single

Oct. 9. George Pattinson of Yoxford singleman and Elizabeth Engall widow, by License

1793. Sep. 12. Thomas Crisp of Walpole singleman and Elizabeth Gosling widow

1794. April 1. John Ludbrooke of Chediston and Elizabeth Strowger both single, by License

1795. April 19. John Clark and Kerenhappuch Smith both single

Oct. 19. Jeremiah Broom and Ann Bullen

1797. April 20. Robert Moore and Sarah Knights both single

1798. Dec. 24. James Spicer bachelor and Lydia Woodgate spinster

1799. March 28. Richard Woodgate widower and Rachel Wright spinster

1800. Aug. 1. Isaac Adams of Hinton and Jane Strowger of Bramfield, by License

1800.	Oct. 8.	James Fisher of Theberton and Mary Peake
1801.	Jan. 21.	Robert Webb of Wenhaston widower and Martha Strowger singlewoman, by License
	Feb. 2.	Nathaniel Briggs of Wissett bachelor and Theresa Peak spinster, by License
1802.	May 26.	John Wink of Darsham and Honour Nolloth singlewoman
	July 26.	George Howlett of Darsham and Ann Crisp both single
	Sep. 18.	Thomas Girling a minor and Sarah Strowger spinster, with consent of Wm Girling the father, by License
1803.	Nov. 8.	David Smith of Cratfield and Martha Peak both single, by License
1804.	Feb. 10.	John Adams and Sarah Wade both single, by License
	Aug. 20.	James Sprat and Mary Gooch both single
1806.	May 9.	Robert Edments and Sarah Reynolds of Rumburg both single, by License
1807.	June 30.	Benjamin Aldridge and Mary Wright both single
1808.	March 24.	James Mills and Ann Knights both single
1809.	Oct. 12.	Thomas Aldrid and Lucy Cole both single
	Nov. 28.	Richard Woodgate and Letitia Smith both single
1811.	April 12.	John Smith widower and Rebecca Haward of Heveningham widow
1812.	Dec. 18.	John Hammant of Bramfield and Sarah Finch both single

Here ends the Second Volume of Marriages.

1814.	Feb. 23.	William Beddingfield and Sarah Girling both single
	Aug. 22.	James Woodgate and Sarah Driver both single
	Oct. 13.	Martin Cuddon and Rhoda Linder both single
	Nov. 11.	Joseph Sheppard and Mary Smith both single, by License
	Nov. 29.	William Coltrop and Elizabeth Haylock both single
	Dec. 27.	Thomas Burgess and Mary Lines both single, by License
1815.	July 27.	James Button and Hannah Ellis both single
1818.	Oct. 27.	William Etheridge of Westleton and Margaret Buckingham both single
	Nov. 3.	Robert Westgate and Mary Ann Dix both single
	Dec. 2.	David Mayhew and Elizabeth Lines both single
1819.	Aug. 3.	John Todd and Honour Ashford both single
1820.	Jan. 20.	Samuel Edwards and Sarah Woodgate both single
1821.	Nov. 23.	William Row and Susan Fisher both single
1822.	Jan. 2.	George Smith of Bramfield and Mary Raven both single
	Sep. 29.	Robert Rawlinson and Sarah Lines both single
1823.	Aug. 5.	Richard Girling widower and Elizabeth Aldrich spinster
1825.	Feb. 2.	John Raven and Sarah Durrant both single
	April 1.	Charles Howard and Sarah Bailey both single
	Oct. 12.	John Browne and Elizabeth Cole both single
1827.	May 15.	James Friend and Mary Rix both single
	May 15.	John Clark and Lydia Bruning both single

1827.	Nov. 28.	Samuel Philpot and Phillis Finch both single
1831.	Jan. 10.	Daniel Hart and Charlotte Aldis both single, by License
	June 29.	James Holden of Walton and Elizabeth Sarah Whiting both single, by License
1832.	March 31.	Thomas Clark of Blythburgh and Susan Spall both single
	July 19.	Robert Tacon of Wissett and Anne Whiting both single, by License
1834.	Sep. 25.	James Lay of Carlton Colville and Susannah Aldis both single, by License

Here ends the Third Volume of Marriages.

1837.	Oct. 12.	William Burrows and Maria Pitcher both single
1838.	July 11.	Thomas Higham of Bramfield, farmer, widower and Martha Davy spinster, by License
1839.	Aug. 8.	James Aldis, 65, farmer, widower and Mary Aldis, 56, widow, by License
1841.	Aug. 10.	John Clarke and Harriet Freeman both single
1842.	May 24.	David Mills, 24, and Matilda Noy, 20, both single
	Nov. 10.	John Mills, 22, and Susannah Rolleston, 20, both single
1843.	Oct. 12.	John Mills, 28, and Faith Hensby, 27, both single
1847.	Nov. 25.	John Geater, 30, miller, of Levington, and Betsy Appleton, 26, both single, by License
1848.	Oct. 13.	John Savage and Betsy Woodgate both single
1849.	Dec. 18.	Henry Youngs, grocer, of Wenhaston and Mary Anne Le Francois both single, by License
1850.	Sep. 16.	William Fulcher of Lowestoft and Mary Ann Haylock both single
1851.	March 14.	Thomas Farmelo and Rachel Raven both single, by License
	Oct. 15.	Daniel Mills and Susan Newson both single
1852.	July 6.	John Noy, 32, of Leiston and Sarah Greenland, 32, both single
1853.	Oct. 12.	John Knights, 28, and Sarah Saker of Blythburgh, 24, both single
	Oct. 12.	John Gayfer, 24, and Elizabeth Saker, 20, of Blythburgh, both single
	Dec. 26.	William Howard, 26, and Hannah Skeet, 23, both single
1854.	Oct. 2.	Samuel Betts Catling, 37, farmer, and Emily Lines, 37, of Wickham Market, both single, by License
1855.	Nov. 23.	William Noy, 29, son of the Parish Clerk, and Mary Ann Eaves, 33, both single
1857.	March 9.	John Moor, 30, of Leiston and Rachel Newson both single
1858.	March 8.	Harvey Peake, 21, farmer, and Martha Harper, 22, both single
	Dec. 27.	George Petitt, 22, of Melton and Maria Rouse, 26, both single
1861.	Jan. 17.	George Smith and Mary Ann Lane both single
	April 27.	James Finch widower and Sarah Edwards widow
	Oct. 8.	Henry Baldry and Mary Ann Stannard both single
1862.	Jan. 28.	William Cooper, 22, and Emma Saker, 15, both single

1863.	April 21.	George Knights of Wenhaston widower and Mary Ann Saker spinster
	May 26.	William Nolloth of Wenhaston and Mary Ann Everson both single
1864.	May 21.	George Kerridge, 23, of Bramfield and Julia Nolloth, 20, both single
	Oct. 13.	Robert Saker and Elizabeth Hunebell both single
1865.	May 31.	James Harvey Peak, farmer, and Esther Elizabeth Andrews both single
	July 3.	James Arman of Lowestoft and Ann Eliza Smith both single
1866.	June 19.	Henry Drew widower and Elizabeth Bennett spinster
	Aug. 6.	Samuel Gilbert widower and Sarah Eade widow
1867.	Jan. 8.	Walter Canham of Wenhaston and Rachel Saker both single
	Sep. 30.	John Lines of Halesworth and Julina Clarke both single
1869.	June 8.	Henry Lane and Lucy Batho both single
	July 13.	Simon Cooper and Ann Carver of Wenhaston both single
	Dec. 25.	William Blazer widower and Elizabeth Andrews widow
1870.	April 14.	John Haylock bachelor and Harriet Pearl of Blythburgh widow
	April 14.	John Fenn and Susan Haylock both single
1872.	May 22.	Edward Roberts and Emma Marjoram both single
1873.	Dec. 30.	James Ablett and Louisa Levirs both single
1874.	Oct. 15.	John Newson and Caroline Eade both single
	Nov. 12.	Charles Friend of Halesworth and Anna Howard a minor both single
	Nov. 26.	William Clements of Halesworth, 20, and Margaret Roberts, 23, both single
1875.	July 7.	Edward Miles of Wenhaston and Eliza Flatt, 20, both single
1876.	June 6.	John Haylock widower and Harriet Canham spinster
	July 6.	A memorandum that Miss Bence [Agnes Marian] was married to Percy Trower, Esq., on July 6, 1876, at S⁺ James's Church, Piccadilly
1878.	Dec. 23.	Albert Haward, 25, of Halesworth and Elizabeth Eade, 21, both single
1879.	Jan. 15.	George Upcraft, 23, of Southwold and Elizabeth Mayhew, 23, both single
	April 28.	Charles Edward Pearce, 23, of Wenhaston and Mary Elizabeth Gilbert, 21, both single
	Oct. 8.	Arthur George Sarbutt, 23, of Ringsfield and Mary Gibbs, 25, both single
	Oct. 28.	George Mills, 25, and Jane Flatt, 20, both single
1880.	Dec. 21.	George Noy, 24, and Esther Mills, 25, both single
1881.	June 6.	Alfred Catchpole, 20, and Elizabeth Gibbs, 18, both single

The following extract from Lecky's " History of England in the Eighteenth Century,"
Vol. I., pp. 490-1, refers to the Marriage Act of 1753.

"The long list of social reforms passed under the Pelham Ministry may be fitly closed by the Marriage Act of Lord Hardwicke, which put a stop to those Fleet marriages, which had become one of the strongest scandals of English life. Before this Act the Canon Law was in force in England, and according to its provisions the mere consent of the parties, followed by cohabitation, constituted, for many purposes, a valid marriage, and a valid marriage for all purposes could be celebrated by a Priest in Orders at any time or place, without registration, and without the consent of parents or guardians. Stamped licences were, indeed, required by law, but not for the validity of the contract, and their omission was only punished as a fraud on the revenue. In such a state of the law atrocious abuses had grown up. A multitude of clergymen, usually prisoners for debt, and almost always men of notoriously infamous lives, made it their business to celebrate clandestine marriages in or near the Fleet. [*The Fleet was a prison in which debtors were confined.*] They performed the ceremony without licence or question, sometimes without even knowing the names of the persons they united, in public-houses, brothels, or garrets. They acknowledged no ecclesiastical superior. Almost every tavern or brandy-shop in the neighbourhood had a Fleet parson in its pay. Notices were placed in the windows, and agents went out in every direction to solicit the passers-by. A more pretentious, and, perhaps, more popular establishment, was the chapel in Curzon Street, where the Rev. Alexander Keith officiated. He was said to have made a 'very bishopric of revenue' by clandestine marriages; and the expression can hardly be exaggerated if it be true, as was asserted in Parliament, that he had married on an average 6000 couples every year. He himself stated that he had married many thousands, the great majority of whom had not known each other more than a week, and many only a day or half a day. Young and inexperienced heirs fresh from college, or even from school, were thus continually entrapped. . . . . . . Among the more noted instances of clandestine marriages we find that of the Duke of Hamilton with Miss Gunning, that of the Duke of Kingston with Miss Chudleigh, that of Henry Fox with the daughter of the Duke of Richmond. . . . . . . It is not surprising that contracts so lightly entered into should have been as lightly violated. Desertion, conjugal infidelity, bigamy, fictitious marriages celebrated by sham priests, were the natural and frequent consequences of the system. In many cases in the Fleet Registers names were suppressed or falsified, and marriages fraudulently ante-dated, and many households, after years of peace, were convulsed by some alleged pre-contract or clandestine tie. It was proved on one occasion before Parliament that there had been 2954 Fleet marriages in four months, and it appeared from the memorandum books of Fleet parsons that one of them made £57 in marriage fees in a single month, that another had married 173 couples in a single day."

P. 498.—"With large classes of the community the easy process of Fleet marriages were very popular. On the day before the new law came into force no less than 300 were celebrated, and a bold attempt was made by a clergyman named Wilkinson to perpetuate the system at the Savoy. He claimed, by virtue of some old privileges attaching to that quarter, to be extra-parochial, and to have the right of issuing licences himself, and he is said to have actually celebrated as many as 1400 clandestine marriages after the Marriage Act had passed. By the instrumentality of Garrick, one of whose company had been married in this manner in 1756, a Savoy licence passed into the hands of the Government, and the trial and transportation of Wilkinson* and his curate put an end to clandestine marriages in England. Those who desired them, however, found a refuge in Scotland [*Gretna Green marriages were made illegal in 1856*]; the Isle of Man [*clandestine marriages were made illegal in the Isle of Man in 1757*] and Guernsey; and in 1760 there were always vessels ready at Southampton to carry fugitive lovers to the latter island." [*The charge for the passage was five guineas.*]

In 1823 another Marriage Act was passed, of which the chief points of difference from that of 1753, are—

That seven days' notice of banns shall be given to the clergyman before the first publication.

That no clergyman shall be punishable by ecclesiastical censures for solemnizing marriages without consent of parents unless he has had notice of such dissent.

That banns must be republished if the marriage is not solemnized within three months.

That no marriage shall be solemnized at any other time than between the hours of eight and twelve in the forenoon.

That when marriage is solemnized between parties under age by false oath or fraud, the guilty party shall forfeit all property accruing from the marriage.

The penalty of transportation for fourteen years for improperly solemnizing marriage was preserved, but the prosecution must take place within three years after the offence was committed.

---

* Wilkinson was transported for some years, and "John Grierson, the clergyman of the Savoy Chapel," was transported for fourteen years for this illegality in 1755. Perhaps he was Dr. Wilkinson's curate.

BURIALS.

(*Robertus Golde, Rector Ecclesiæ de Thorington*, 1593.)

1594.	Jan. 21.	Elizabeth Donnet wife of Anthonie Donnet
	Feb. 2.	Mary Wiseman wife of John Wiseman
1595.	April 22.	Marye Randall servant to Edward Coke Esquire the Queenes Attourny Generall
	May 3.	Dorothie Johnson wife of Thomas Johnson
	Oct. 27.	Thomas Robertsone servant to Edward Coke Esquire the Queenes Attourny Generall
1596.		nulla
1597.	May 13.	Rose Silvester
1598.	Jan. 26.	Henry Thurston servant to Henry Crispe
1599.	April 3.	Thomas Johnson soune of Thomas Johnson and Elizabeth his wife
1600.	Nov. 16.	Roberte Tayler sonne of Richard Tailer of Bliborough beinge founde drowned about Kratsall bridge in Thorington. [*The name of Kratsall bridge is not now known.*]
1601.	Jan. 30.	Elizabeth Bartelet wife of Richarde Bartelet
1602.	Jan. 25.	Roger Alden soone of John Alden and Em'e his wife
1603.	June 27.	Henry Crispe
1604.		nulla
1605.	April 6.	John Aldinge
1606.	May 7.	John Reave servannt to ffrancis Seppens
	May 10.	Elizabeth Crampton gentlewoman*

* *On the last page of the first Book of Registers are the following entries:—*

Septembris 20, 1607.

Memorandum, vzt. Richard Crampton and John Crampton executours of the Last Will and testam' of M'rs Elizabeth Crampton their sister did the daye and yeare abone written deliver into the handes of Thomas Johnson and Edwarde Foxe then Churchwardinges of Thorington the som'e of five pownde of Lawefull English mony given by the said Elizabeth to the poore inhabitants of the aforesaid Towne of Thorington to be a continweall stocke to be imployed for the said poore people. Robte Golde.

1607.

Thomas Johnson one of the Churchwardens did at the feast of St. Michaell the Archangle 1607 take the aforesaid five powndes into his handes and promised freely to the inhabitants of the said towne for one yeares use thereof ten shillinges w'ch som'e of xs he performed and paid the 2'th of October 1608 in the presence of Paule Golde Robte Golde George Spaldinge.

1608.

The saide Thomas Johnson retayneth in his handes the said five powndes for another yeare vdz. from the feast of St. Michaell the Archangle 1608 vnto the said feast next insweing w'th like promise of payinge x' as before—which said x' the said Thomas Johnson paid the xvii'th of December 1609 into the bands of ffrancye Seppens Churchwarden in the p'sence of Roberte

1607.	May 26.	William Alding sonne of John Aldinge and Em'e his wife
	July 10.	Elizabeth Emans daughter of George Emans and Dyonis his wife
	Dec. 28.	Ellen Dawson
	Jan. 17.	Jane Spaldinge daughter of George Spaldinge and Sarah his wife
1608.		nulla
1609.	May 6.	Elizabeth Spaldinge daughter of Richard Spaldinge and Percy his wife
	June 4.	Isabell Seppens widdowe
1610.	Aug. 5.	George Emans
	Sep. 30.	Mr Paule Golde*
	Dec. 10.	Dyonis Emans widdowe
1611.	June 26.	Alice Crispe widdowe
1612.	Sep. 11.	Thomas Nuttall
	Nov. 26.	The widdowe Christian ffellowe
1613.	June 25.	Richarde Bartlett
1614.	Feb. 14.	Elizabeth Nichols daughter of Willia' Nichols and Katharine his wife
	Dec. (—)	John West
1615.	Aug. 20.	Dorcas Reve daughter of Thomas Reve and Elizabeth his wife
	June 23.	Edward Cartwright singleman
1616.	July 10.	John Elvine singleman
	Jan. 12.	ffrances Seppens
1617.	Aug. 8.	William Bloyse sonne of Philippe Bloys and Alice his wife
	Jan. 29.	Elizabeth Wiseman wiffe of John Wiseman
1618.	March 28.	Richarde foxe
	May 25.	Elizabeth Lowe daughter of Henry Lowe and Vnica his wife
1620.	July 13.	Robart Golde Rector of Thorington ætat. 62. [*M.I.* See Institutions, 1593, 1609, 1612]†

Golde John Lewes and others and the said xª was uppon Christmas daye next after dystributed amonge the poore people of Thorington in the psence of the said Robte Golde John Lewes George Spaldinge John Letton and others.

1609.

The said Thomas Johnson reteyneth in his hand the said five pownds for another whole yeare, yet. from the feast of the nativity of Crist 1609 to the said feast next insweinge with like promise of payinge xª as before. Witnesses Robert Golde ffrancys Seppens George Spalding John Letton.

The said Thomas Johnson with the consent of the rest off the towne did paye the sd five pownds to Raynold Lassy for a perce of land to the vse of the poore.

The first mention in the Churchwarden's accounts of the possession of a piece of land is in the year 1720-21, as follows:—" Rec't one yeares Rentt for yᵉ church pice due at Easter 1720 10'," which sum was applied to the payment of the Churchwarden's expenses.

---

* From Davy's MSS. *In Thorington in the time of K. James Robert Gold Bachelour in Divinity was Rector and Paul Gold Dr. of Physick his younger brother lived also in that parish and both of them died s.p.*

† *Extract from the will (dated 1592, and proved at Norwich 1595) of Anne Bedingfield, widow, who married, 1st, Nicholas Arrowsmith, of Huntingfield Hall; 2udly, John Paston, by whom she was mother of Bridget, first wife of Edward (afterwards Sir Edward) Coke; and 3rdly, Edmund Bedingfield.* "Item I give to Robert Goulde, Clerke, £10 for the great pains and diligent care he hath had and will have over my said grandchild Edward Coke to be paid to

BURIALS. 71

1620.	Dec. 17.	ffrances Stacy daughter of James Stacy and Alice his wife
1621.	April 15.	Susan White
1622.	April 1.	Bridget Coke daughter of Arthur Coke Esquire and Elizabeth his wife [*See note, p. 23*]
	April 14.	Thomas Feltham sonne of Harbonne Feltham and Muriell his wife [*See note, p. 24*]
	Aug. 23.	John Gilney
1623.	April 28.	John Wiseman
1624.	March 22.	Jane Blois wyf to Master Blois citizen of Norwich
	Jan. 26.	Edward Foxe
1625.	Aug. 30.	Elizabeth Bartlet widow
	Sep. 7.	Rose West widow
	Jan. 15.	Reginald Murdocke sone of William Murdook and Susane his wife
1626.	(——)	francis Gillinghame sone of Alise Gillinghame
	Aug. 7.	Mary felthame daughter of Harborne Felthame, gent., and Muriel his wife [*Bap. May 11, 1625*]
	Sep. 16.	John Litton
1627.	Sep. 25.	Elizabeth wife of John ffreeman, Clarke. [*A daughter Elizabeth was baptized the same day. The first entry made in John Freeman's handwriting is this of his wife. He signs the bottom of the page as John ffreeman, Curate. He was buried 1656.*]
1628.	Oct. 28.	Em'e Moulton daughter of Edmond Moulton and Julyan his wife
	Dec. 10.	Tamasin wif of William Bends
	Dec. 21.	Margeret Ewered widdowe
	Jan. 14.	Martha wife of James Clyforde
1629.	June 26.	Marye Alds daughter of Richard Aldus and Marye his wife
	Oct. 21:	Margaret daughter of Samuell Garrould and Margaret his wife
1630.	June 13.	Jane Lovelace, widdowe alive the wife of Richard Lovelace Esquire (M.I.)*
	Aug. 27.	Parnell daughter of John Tockley and Rose his wife
	Dec. 21.	Robert sonne of Henry Coke Esquire and Margaret his wife [*Bap. Aug. 24, 1629*]
	Jan. 14.	Katharine ffoxe widdowe

him by the hands of my executors." *She also bequeathed "10ᵉ a year to be paid by my executors to the poor people inhabiting or dwelling in the town of Thorington for and during the said term of ten years."*

Davy's MSS, Bramfield, fol. 129. *"In Bramfield, Robert Gold, Rector of Thorington, had an estate which (dying without issue) he gave to Arthur Coke, Esq., one of the sonnes of Sir Edward Coke, sometime L. Chiefe Justice. The widow of Mr. Gold had it for her life: her second husband was .... Blosse, Alderman of Norwich."* Thomas Blose and Jane Gold were married at Westleton 15th October, 1622. Query, Were these the same? For her burial see *March* 22, 1624.

* *The Lovelaces first appear at Bethersden, Kent, about 1368. They acquired property also at Kingsdown, Bayford Castle in Sittingbourne, Canterbury, and in London. All sprang from the same stock, from which also came the Lords Lovelace of Hurley, co. Berks, whose peerage became extinct in 1736. Extract from the will (proved 3rd August, 1630) of Jane Lovelace, of*

1630.	Feb. 8.	William Bends
1631.	April 19.	Thomas Coke son'e of Henrye Coke Esquire and Margaret his wife [*Bap.* 27 *Oct.* 1630]
	July 24.	Margaret Cherisson wife of John Cherisson
1632.	Dec. 2.	Grace Rumsby wife of Nicholas Rumsby
1633.	Jan. 9.	Joane Ellys
1634.	June 17.	Marye wife of Thomas Amys
	Feb. 9.	John Gosling
1636.	April 17.	Rachel wife of Robt. Leggate
	Sep. 14.	ffrancis son'e of Richard and Mary Aldus
	Nov. 18.	ffrances Barthlet
	Dec. 20.	Thomas son'e of William and Prudence Cone
	Feb. 7.	ffrancis Seppens
1637.	May 30.	Katharine daughter of James and Elizabeth Presson
	Nov. 29.	Lidia Wells singlewoman
	Feb. 16.	Olyfe wife of Robert Haward
1638.	June 22.	Harborne ffeltham, gent. [*See note, p.* 24
	Sep. 27.	Edward Mihills
	Oct. 22.	Rose wife of John Tockly
	Oct. 26.	Marye Haward
1639.	March 30.	William Scot
	June 12.	Marye Swinborne
	Oct. 26.	Marye wife of Richard Aldus
	Feb. 19.	Alice wife of Robt. ffella
1640.	July 25.	James Presson
	Dec. 23.	Henrye Scot
1641.	June 25.	Elizabeth wine of John Smyth
	Aug. 9.	Alice daughter of Thom Scotte and Katheren his wine
	Sep. 22.	Elizabeth daughter of Robt. Browne and Ann his wine
	Oct. 20.	Thom son of Thom Scotte and Katheren his wine
	Nov. 11.	Ann daughter of Robt. Browne and Ann his wine
	Dec. 31.	Elizabeth Presson wine of James Presson
	Jan. 8.	Francis son of Robt. Browne and Anne his wine
	Jan. 19.	Richard Alldus
	Jan. 26.	Adry Scotte
	March 8.	Willm. Burnete
1642.	March 30.	Jane Coke daughter of Henry Coke Esqr. and Margeret his wine [*Bap.* April 28, 1628]
	Dec. 24.	Elizabeth and Margaret Groome her daughter
1643.	Dec. 22.	Vere ffiske
1644.	March 29.	Joh. Durrant

1645.	Jan. 16.	Tho. ffiske
1653.	Nov. 8.	Catren Scote wife of Thomas Scote wos Beared
	Feb. 20.	John Collet son of francis Collet and Anne his wife wose Bevried
	March 10.	Ann Collet wife of francis Collet wose bevried
1654.	March 26.	Edmond Dorent son of John Dorent and Mary his wife wose bevried
	May 10.	Margry Sepenes wido. wos bevried
	Sep. 19.	Robrt. Durant was bevried
	Oct. 27.	Robert ffelloe was bevried
1655.	March 20.	Matha Seppenes daughter of ffrancis Seppenes and Matha his wife
1656.	July 13.	John Seppenes
	Oct. 28.	Robrt. Borwred was Bearred
	Feb. 17.	Susane Durante wido was burede
	March 22.	John freman, Clarke [*His wife was buried Sept.* 25, 1627. *See note, p.* 71]
1657.	May 29.	Willam Seppenes
1658.	Jan. 6.	Elizabeth Hamond wife of Richard Hamond
	March 3.	Willam Sampsone
1659.	July 22.	John Chunn, Clarke [*See Institutions*, 1646]
1661.	Nov. 19.	Henary Coke, Esqe. [*5th son of Sir Edward Coke*]*
	Dec. 28.	Robrt. Coke sone of Hinary Coke, Esqe. [*Bap. Nov.* 27, 1634]
1662.	June 25.	Thomas Larke sone of Willam Larke
	July 12.	Matha Seppenes wife of ffrancis Seppenes
1663.	Jan. 19.	Grace Blowres
	Nov. 19.	John Smith
	Feb. 13.	Thomas Wood
1677.	Dec. 16.	Mathew wife of William Cone
1678.	Dec. 23.	Olive daughter of Herman and Rebakah Attwood
	Dec. 28.	Rebecca daughter of Hermon and Rebecca Attwood both of which were bound in wollen according to law [*See note, p.* 29]†
	Jan. 27.	Thomas flisk

* MSS. of Suffolk Families. Conder. p. 456 : " In Thorington this year 1655 liveth Henry Coke, Esq., one of the sonnes of Sir Edward Coke. Knt. sometime Lord Chiefe Justice; his estate £1500 or £2000 per ann."

† In 1666 an Act was passed " to encourage the woollen manufacture of this kingdom," by which it was ordered that the dead should be buried in woollen only. The friends of the deceased were required to make an affidavit that this had been done, and the affidavit was to be presented to the officiating clergyman. This Act was repealed by 30 Car. II., St. i., c. 3, and by 32 Car. II., c. 1. These latter Acts were repealed by 54 Geo. III., c. 108.

Copy of a Certificate under the Act for Burying in Woollen.

(From the " Diocesan Registry, Norwich.")

Suff. Southwold. April 26, 1690.

These are to certifie y* Anne Burnet in Walderswick, in the county forsd, came before mee y* day aboresd, and made affidavit upon oath. in p'nce of those whose names are hereunto sett, y* Elisabeth, y* wife of Andrew Lillie, in the abovenamed parish and county, lately deceasd there, was buried in the ordinarie burying place thereof, being wound, wrapt up, and layd foorth, in

L

1678.	Feb. 7.	ffrances ffisk
1679.	Aug. 2.	Cyriack Coke*
	Sep. 2.	Rebekah Evans†
1680.	March 30.	Margret Durrant
	April 4.	Georg Evans sonne of John and Matthew Evans
	Oct. 6.	Elizabeth Youngs
	Oct. 13.	Laurence sonne of John and Anne Mayhew [See note, p. 29]
	Oct. 17.	Thomas sonne of John Mayhew, Clerk, and Anne his wife
	Nov. 30.	Edmond Rabbit [See note, p. 28]
	Feb. 16.	Martha Taylor daughter of Willm Taylor of Walderswick
1681.	March 25.	Anne daughter of John Wade
	April 9.	Martha wife of Robt. Smith
	Dec. 24.	John Evans
1682.	May 6.	Edmond ffeltham, Gent. [See note, p. 24]
	Jan. 6.	Mary ffella, widdw.
	Feb. 14.	John Lodge
	Feb. 24.	Thomas sonne of Thomas Scott
	June 15.	ffrancis Rabbit, widdow [See note, p. 28]
1683.	April 14.	Robert Twaits son of Samuel Twaits
	April 15.	Margret Larke, widdow
	Sep. 3.	Anne Mayhew daughter of John Mayhew, Clerke, and Anne his wife [See note, p. 29]
1688.	Nov. 28.	Thomas sonne of John Mayhew, Clerke, and Anne his wife
1693.	Sep. 28.	John Mayhew, Reev of this parish and Holton [See Institutions, 1676. M.I.]
1695.	July 7.	Elizabeth daughter of Thomas Scot and Elizabeth his wife
1696.	Oct. 11.	ffrances Scot, widow
	Oct. 24.	Henry son of Thomas Layston, labourer, and Mary his wife
1697.	April 4.	George ffuller, sexton
	May 1.	Mary Smith, widow
	Jan. 26.	Elizabeth daughter of John Pallant and Mary his wife
	Jan. 31.	John Miller, yeoman
1698.	Nov. 27.	Jonathan son of John Pallant
1698/9.	Feb 16.	Elizabeth daughter of John Pallant
	Mar. 24.	Ann daughter of Tho. Layson

woollen only, and no other material then what is made of sheeps wool only : accordinge to ye Act of Parlia't. made for burying in woollen only.

Witnesses, Barbara Petre,   Jurat' coram me
          Katrine Petre.   Ja. Petre, mir of So'wold.

* In 1627 Henry Coke, Esq., son of Sir Ed. Coke, granted to Mary Man and Margaret Man daughters of William Man and Mary his wife, one cottage and garden adjoining measuring about one acre, in the parish of Thorington, because of her good and carefull nursing of his son Cirioe and his daughter Brigitte. Davy's MSS., Court Rolls.

† Probably widow of the late Rector, William Evans. See Marriages, 1665. He was a resident Rector. He makes his first entry of marriages in 1661, and signs his name at the bottom of the page, and all entries thenceforward to 1675 are in his handwriting. He died in 1676, but there is no entry of any burial between the years 1663 and 1667 : so his burial, if it took place here, is not noticed.

1700.	April 25.	Mary daughter of Francis Watling
	Sep. 30.	Hannah daughter of Thos. Laysone and Mary his wife
	Jan. 3.	Wᵐ Gray
1701.	April 17.	Martha daughter of Thomas Scot, labourer
	Dec. 5.	Edward son of Edward Darby and Elizabeth his wife
1702.	Jan. 5.	Robt. son of Nich. Ewen
1703-4.	Feb. 9.	Thomas Layson, sexton
1705-6.	Feb. 8.	Margrett daughter of Roger Burwood
	March 13.	Mary daughter of Samᵈ Stoger
1708.	Nov. 2.	Mary wife of William Blowers
1710-11.	Feb. 4.	Nicholas Ewin
	March 12.	Richard Turner
1715.	April 8.	William son of William Lamb
1716.	Dec. 28.	Mary wife of William Goodall, who was found dead in yᵉ fields going from Halesworth
1716-17.	March 9.	John son of Thoˢ Cook
1720.	Oct. 13.	Hannah Burward
	Feb. 3.	Roger Burward
1721.	Oct. 4.	Ann Mayhu [widow of the late Rector. M.I.]
	Feb. 21.	Mary wife of John French
	March 19.	Samuel Strogier
1722.	April 17.	Hannah French
	Nov. 3.	Samuell Austin
1723.	Nov. 27.	James son of James Barker and Mary his wife
1723-4.	March 9.	Thomas Scott of this parish
1724-5.	Jan. 20.	Elizebeth Watling
1725.	April 4.	Richard Lamb
	June 19.	John Adams of Cratfield
	July 7.	Hannah wife of Abraham Blowers
1726.	June 30.	Elisabeth wife of Alexander Bloss
	Aug. 14.	William Harvy, an infant
1727.	Sep. 3.	Thomas Grice
	Nov. 1.	Mary wife of William Burward
1728.	April 7.	William son of Thomas and Mary Rimington
	May 31.	Elizabeth daughter of William and Anne Harvy
	Aug. 3.	Sarah Harvy, an infant
	Oct. 15.	Temperance Grice
	Oct. 2.	Mary wife of Robert Jackson, of Yoxford
1728-9.	Feb. 23.	Anne daughter of Jonathan Reed
1729.	Aug. 13.	William Goodall
	Aug. 24.	Frances Turner, widdow
	Dec. 14.	Thomas base son of Thomas Bliss and Mary Meen
	March 22.	Susan of Mary Crisp
	March 29.	Philip of Philip Strowger
1730.	July 12.	Anne wife of William Harvy
1730-1.	Jan. 21.	Jane daughter of William and Mary Lurwood
	Jan. 24.	Margett daughter of John Spooner and Margett his wife

1730-1.	Jan. 24.	Elizebeth daughter of George Berry and Elizebeth his wife
1731.	July 14.	Dorothy Watling of the parish of Bramfield
	Oct. 13.	Daniell son of George Berry and Elizebeth his wife
1732.	April 4.	Eliz. daughter of Jane Stroger and Philip her husband
	Sep. 10.	Elizebeth Stroger, widdow
1733-4.	Feb. 25.	Abraham Blowers
1734.	Oct. 9.	Elizebeth daughter of Thomas Rymmiugton
	Feb. 6.	Elizebeth Gale
1735.	Sep. 24.	Francis Watlin
1736.	Feb. 2.	Henry son of Henry and Elizabeth Brown
1737.	March 29.	George Berry
	July 12.	Anne Baxter
	Sep. 18.	Mary Pells
1738.	June 20.	Hanna Turpin of Westhall
	Oct. 29.	Judah Knoller, widow
	March 1.	Robert Riches, an infant, of Wenhaston
1739.	Jan. 27.	Sarah Jarves, an infant
	Feb. 17.	Jonathan Ball, a married man
1740.	May 11.	John Tyrrell, an infant
	Oct. 5.	Ann wife of Alexander Bloss
1741.	Jan. 6.	Gregory Adams ; by Mr Leech
1742.	June 7.	Alexander Bence, Junr, Esquire [M.I. See Pedigree]
	July 30.	Lydia Solomon, an infant
1743-4-5.		None
1746.	May 28.	James Stronger, an infant
	Oct. 18.	Elizabeth French
1747-8.	Jan. 2.	Sarah Docking, an infant
1748.	Dec. 13.	John Tyrrell, a lad
1749.	May 31.	John Docking, an infant
1750.	July 29.	John Docking, an infant
	Aug. 5.	Joseph Head
1751.	June 30.	Sarah Simons, an infant
	Sep. 17.	Susannah Carver
	Nov. 8.	Elizabeth Field [M.I.]
1752.	May 14.	Sarah Symonds
	Dec. 8.	John French
1753.	Feb. 13.	Robert Foulgham
	Sep. 2.	Alexander Bloss
1754.	Jan. 6.	Mary Turner
	May 10.	Mary Rymmington
	May 23.	Francis Docking [M.I.]
1755.	May 13.	Elizabeth Leatherdale
1756.	June 17.	Mrs Mary Bence [M.I. See Pedigree]
1757.	May 10.	John Goddard, an infant
	May 29.	Philip Stronger
	June 30.	Elizabeth Woodgate, an infant
1758.	April 21.	Elizabeth wife of Robert Spore

1759.	Aug. 8.	Alexander Bence, Esq. [M.I. *See Pedigree*]
1760.	(——)	James of William and Mary Woodyard
1761.	Feb. 20.	Mrs Margaret Bishop, spinster [M.I.]
	April 11.	Susannah daughter of Richard and Ann Woodgate
	Dec. 2.	Richard Crowfoot, boarder with Saml Strowger
1762.	Dec. 12.	Robt of Robt and Margaret Shade
1763.	April 29.	Susannah daughter of Richard and Ann Woodgate
	Aug. 1.	Ann wife of Thos Cole
	Aug. 20.	Elizabeth wife of Robert Hicham
	Sep. 13.	Willm of Robert (Junr) and Marg^t Spore
1764.	May 31.	Thomas Rimmington
	June 28.	Francis Dorkins, from Raydon [M.I.]
1765.	Nov. 19.	Elizabeth of Henry and Hannah Briggs
1766.	July 8.	Robert Manning, servant to Geo. Golding, Esq., drown'd in bathing
	Aug. 16.	Daniel Strowger
1767.	March 12.	Mary Barker the Clerk's d^r
1768.	Jan. 19.	John Smith, serv^t to P. Strowger
	July 31.	James of James and Jemmima Newson
	Aug. 20.	Elizabeth wife of John Baxter
1769.	Feb. 22.	Thos. Letherdale
	June 3.	Wm Haward
	Aug. 11.	Elisabeth Nolloth, widow
1772.	Jan. 27.	Rosanna Briggs, infant
	March 22.	Jane Strowger, widow
	July 10.	William of William and Elizth Roberts
	Aug. 19.	Henry Veal, labourer, kill'd by a colt
	Dec. 3.	James James, farmer [M.I.]
1773.	Feb. 21.	Christopher Jarvis, labourer
1778.	May 24.	Sarah (infant) of James and Sarah Balls
1779.	Nov. 4.	Elizabeth widow of James James
	Nov. 11.	Mary Mouser, widow
1780.	March 1.	Esther daughter of Rich^d and Ann Woodgate
	July 22.	Sarah Jarviss, widow
1781.	Feb. 7.	William Miller (sojourner)
	Feb. 17.	Hannah wife of Saml Studd
	Nov. 1.	Robert Spore, yeoman
1782.	Jan. 13.	Sarah of Robt and Margaret Shade
	Feb. 3.	Robert son of Saml and Sarah Elmy
1783.	March 7.	Robert son of Samuel and Sarah Elmy
	Aug. 20.	Richard of William and Sarah Knights

End of the First Volume of Burials.

	Dec. 31.	Hurstin, base son of Anna Greenwood, accidentally frozen to death
1785.	Nov. 25.	Jonathan, son of Richard Woodgate and Sarah his wife (Sarah Reeve, spinster), aged 2 years

1787. June 17. Charlotte, infant daughter of James Finch and Ann his wife (late Wickerton)

1788. Jan. 27. Ann Woodgate (late Ablet, spinster), wife of Richard Woodgate, aged 68 years

June 15. Sarah, daughter of Samuel Elmy and Sarah his wife (late Jarvis, spinster), aged 22 years

July 22. John, son of Peter Wickerton and Ann his wife (late Green, spinster), aged 16 years

1789. March 28. Richard Woodgate, married man, aged 68

April 19. Richard, infant son of Geo. Nunn and Sarah his wife (late Sarah Baxter, spinster)

1790. March 25. Ann Smith, wife of Eleazar Smith (late Woodgate, spinster), aged 41 years, pauper

1791. Sep. 4. Sarah, wife of William Knights (late Puttock, spinster), aged 39 years [M.I.]

1792. Sep. 21. George Read, single man, of the parish of Framlingham, aged 21 years

July 12. Ann Elmy, daughter of Samuel Elmy and Sarah his wife (late Jarvis, spinster), aged 20 years

1793. Sep. 9. Lydia Elmy, daughter of Samuel Elmy and Sarah his wife, aged 18 years

1794. Oct. 3. Ann Golding, wife of George Golding, Esq., aged 80 years [M.I. See Bence Pedigree]

Dec. 28. John Clarke, married man, aged 70 years

1795. March 7. Thomas Girling, married man, aged 66 years [M.I.]

1796. Jan. 19. Sarah Woodgate, wife of Richard Woodgate, aged 55 years

Oct. 18. Susan Girling, widow, aged 74 years [M.I.]

1797. May 22. Elizabeth Clarke, widow of John Clarke, aged 63

1801. March 29. Samuel Woodgate, son of Rob\u{t} Woodgate and Eliz\u{th} (Mawer) his wife

April 6. James Buckingham, son of Nich\u{s} Buckingham and Mildred (Mabson) his wife, an infant

Nov. 8. George Woodgate, son of Richard Woodgate and Rachael (Wright) his wife

Dec. 24. William Woodgate, aged 47 years, was brought from Wenhaston

1802. March 21. Margaret, wife of Robert Shade, aged 63 years

May 9. Isaac Adams, widower, aged 82 years

June 22. Robert Buckingham, an infant

Oct. 1. Shade's child, a still-born infant

1803. Feb. 3. Robert Butcher, widower, aged 72 years ; by me J. Finch

Feb. 19. William Lines, son of Tho\u{s} and Eliz. Lines, aged 3 years [M.I.]

March 30. Eliz. Wade, aged 79 years

Nov. 2. Susan and Mary Ann Coates, twin daughters of Valentine Coates

Dec. 29. George Golding, Esq., aged 79 years [See Bence Pedigree]

1804. Jan. 1. William Smith, infant

May 11. Robert Woodgate, bachelor, son of Robert and Elizabeth Woodgate, aged 26 years

1804.	June 25.	Ann Brees, single woman, aged 20 years
	July 9.	Philip Stroger, married man, aged 68 years [M.I.]
1806.	June 2.	William Haylock, aged 45 years
	Sep. 25.	Samuel Elmy, aged 70 years
	Oct. 5.	Ann Wickerton, aged 73 years
1807.	April 26.	William Aldis, infant [M.I.]
1808.	April 10.	Mary Shade, aged 3 years
	July 9.	Alban Peak, single man, aged 23 years [M.I.]
	July 30.	Mary Fisher, sister to the above Alban, aged 30 years [M.I.]
	Nov. 23.	Jonathan Webb, infant
1809.	Feb. 9.	William Walker, infant
	Nov. 19.	Bridget Scott
1810.	Feb. 10.	William Peak, aged 66 years [M.I.]
	March 9.	Esther Woodgate, aged 20 years
1811.	March 28.	Hannah Woodgate, aged 2 years
	April 14.	George Nunn, aged 67 years
	June 9.	Harriet Adams of Blythburg, aged 4 years [M.I.]
1812.	Feb. 16.	George Wright, infant
	March 19.	Robert Woodgate, aged 5 years
1811.	Aug. 6.	Jane Adams of Blythburg, aged 31 years [M.I.]
1811.	Dec. 31.	John Adams of Blythburg, aged 2 years

On the last page but one of this Register Book is the following
entry in pencil:

Jonathan Woodgate was buried Ap. 22, 1812, aged 24 years

The Third Book of Registers of Burials.

1813.	Feb. 6.	Sarah Elmy, widow, aged 67
	March 10.	Robert Shade, Bulchamp, aged 79
1815.	April 23.	Anne Aldis, age year old and quarter [M.I.]
	Nov. 3.	Peter Whittaken, aged 83
1816.	Feb. 29.	Elizabeth Woodgate, aged 55
1817.	April 4.	James Goddard Wright, inf.
1818.	March 5.	Valentine Coates, churchwarden, aged 71, died Sat. Feb. 28 [M.I.]
	May 23.	Thomas Lines, aged 54, died Monday 18 May at Ellough [M.I.]
	June 16.	Susan Haylock of Wenhaston, aged 29
	Nov. 2.	Thomas Walker, aged 65, died Tuesday Oct. 27 [M.I.]
	Dec. 31.	John Clark, aged 51, died Friday Dec. 25
1819.	Aug. 15.	John Goddard Wright, aged 1 year
	Sep. 4.	Richard Woodgate, aged 69, died Tuesday Aug. 31
1820.	Feb. 10.	James Girling, aged 18, died Sunday the 6th
	May 20.	Thomas Wilkinson, late of Lambeth near London, aged 54, died Wednesday the 17th
	July 6.	Robert Woodgate, accidentally killed in a pit near the Church by the falls in of gravel, Weds. morn², July 4, aged 66
	Sep. 10.	John Smith, aged 65, died Mon⁷ the 4th

1820.	Sep. 18.	Ann Finch, wife of James Finch, Parish Clerk, aged 54, died Fri. morn. the 15th
1821.	Feb. 1.	Louisa Beddingfield, aged 1 month, died Mon. Jan. 29
	Dec. 29.	Thomas Burgess of Wenhaston, son of Thomas and Mary Burgess, late Lines, aged 2 years [M.I.]
1822.	July 6.	Elizabeth Girling (late Smith), wife of Richard Girling, aged 39 [M.I.]
1823.	Nov. 27.	William Girling, aged 59
1826.	Jan. 13.	Sarah Edmunds, aged 42 [M.I.]
	July 20.	Louisa Adams of Blythborough, aged 9 months
	Nov. 2.	Robert Goodwin, aged 87
1827.	May 29.	James Finch, aged 63
	Oct. 28.	George Rawlinson, an inf[t]
	April 4.	William Noy, aged 2
1828.	March 7.	Ann Raven, aged 58
	Sep. 28.	Susan Girling of Henstead, aged 76 [M.I.]
	Nov. 25.	Margaret Peake, aged 83 [M.I.]
1830.	April 9.	Sarah Breeze, aged 26 [M.I.]
	May 2.	Samuel Stannard, aged 33
	Oct. 13.	William Girling of Henstead, aged 73 [M.I.]
1831.	May 24.	Thomas Butcher, aged 57
	Aug. 22.	Martha Stronger of Wenhaston, aged 94 [M.I.]
	Sep. 14.	James Aldis, aged 23 [M.I.]
1832.	Jan. 24.	Ann Shade of Blythborough, aged 72
	April 25.	Robert James Peake, aged 1 year and 11 months
	Sep. 11.	Mary Ann Smith, aged 32
	Oct. 9.	Chester Smith, an inf[t]
	Dec. 23.	Robert Edments, aged 64 [M.I.]
1833.	May 25.	Marianne Katherine Starkie Bence, aged 15, *only daughter, born and baptized Nov. 2, 1817, at Kelsale, died May 21 at Bracondale, near Norwich* [M.I. *See Pedigree*]
	Aug. 25.	Harriet Spall, aged 18
1834.	Feb. 14.	Ann Aldis, aged 17 [M.I.]
	Sep. 12.	Sophia Newson, aged 41
	Dec. 4.	Elizabeth Lines of Wenhaston, aged 63
1836.	June 11.	Robert Lines, aged 17
	Dec. 29.	William Knights, aged 85 [M.I.]
1837.	April 2.	Robert Rawlinson, aged 36
	Dec. 15.	Marianne Aldis, aged 25 [M.I.]
	Dec. 15.	Martha Aldis, aged 22 [M.I.]
1838.	Jan. 6.	Caroline Aldis, aged 17 [M.I.]
	Jan. 21.	Ann Aldis, aged 60 [M.I.]
	Feb. 9.	Elizabeth Ann Aldis, aged 31 [M.I.]
	Feb. 19.	John Aldis, aged 20 [M.I.]
	April 13.	Eliza Aldis, aged 19 [M.I.]
		These seven of one family all died of fever.
1839.	May 14.	Mary Friend, aged 43 [M.I.]

1841.	Jan. 2.	Sarah Rix, aged 67
	Sep. 19.	Liner Finch, aged 11
	Sep. 30.	Israel Culham of Wenhaston, aged 56
	Oct. 18.	Karenhappuck Clarke of Bulchamp Union House, aged 73
	Nov. 16.	Thomas Lines of Melton Asylum, aged 37 [M.I.]
1842.	Jan. 27.	Joseph Spall, aged 69
	Sep. 27.	Margaret Walker of Wissett, aged 71
1843.	July 22.	James Aldis, aged 69 [M.I.]
	Dec. 25.	Nicholas Buckingham of Wenhaston, aged 81 [M.I.]
1844.	July 26.	Amy Appleton, aged 21 [M.I.]
1846.	Aug. 11.	Sarah Marshlain, aged 51 [M.I.]
	Sep. 12.	Mildred Buckingham of Wreningham, Norfolk, aged 74 [M.I.]
1847.	Sep. 12.	Rachael Page of St. Nicholas, South Elmham, aged 80
1848.	Dec 17.	Mary Spall, aged 72
1851.	June 18.	Peter Whittaker of Bulchamp Union House, aged 81.
1852.	Sep. 21.	Ann Lines of Wickham Market, aged 43 [M.I.]
1853.	April 19.	Thomas Farmelo of Ditchingham, aged 63 [M.I.]
	May 7.	Thomas Gooch Appleton of Halesworth, aged 25
	Dec. 30.	James Rush, aged 13 [M.I.]
1854.	March 18.	Hannah Walker, aged 55 [M.I.]
	March 19.	Rebecca Smith, aged 91
	June 21.	Emma Rawlinson, aged 21
1855.	Feb. 20.	Thomas Girling of Wrentham, aged 73 [M.I.]
	March 15.	Sarah Girling of Wrentham, aged 77 [M.I.]
	March 28.	Susan Rowe, aged 64
	April 16.	Sarah Rawlinson, aged 9 months
	Nov. 20.	Maria Clark, aged 66 [M.I.]
1856.	June 29.	Charles Clode Rowe, aged 2 years and 3 months [M.I.]
	July 1.	Susan Finch, aged 50
	Oct. 16.	Margaret Appleton of Halesworth, aged 21
1857.	March 12.	Catherine Rush of Ipswich, aged 36
	May 16.	Robert Appleton of Halesworth, aged 39
1858.	Jan. 22.	Anne Mills, aged 72
	July 2.	James Friend of Wenhaston, aged 80 [M.I.]
	July 20.	Thomas Starkie Bence, Rector of this Parish, aged 83 [M.I. See Pedigree]
1859.	March 11.	Tabbitha Haylock, aged 64
	Aug. 8.	Robert Appleton of Wenhaston, aged 68 [M.I.]
1860.	June 15.	Martha Peake, aged 26
	Oct. 1.	Edgar Frederick Owles, an infant
1861.	Feb. 16.	Henry Bence Bence, aged 72 [M.I. See Pedigree]
	Feb. 17.	Ann Finch, aged 18
	June 20.	Susan Appleton of Yoxford, aged 66 [M.I.]
	Aug. 16.	James Newson, aged 70
1862.	Nov. 22.	James Peake, aged 73 [M.I.]
	Dec. 27.	Elizabeth Susanna Bence of St. Leonards (late of Thorington), aged 67 [M.I. See Pedigree]

M

1864.	Jan. 24.	William Baldry, aged 10 months
	May 30.	Hedley Fred Owles of London, aged 4 months
	Sep. 7.	George Knights, aged 2 weeks
1865.	Jan. 18.	Mary Walker of Wenhaston, aged 62 [M.I.]
	March 15.	James Mills of Bulchamp, aged 84
	June 19.	Edgar Fred. Owles of Hoxton New Town, London, aged 5 months [M.I.]
	July 21.	Ida Agnes Owles of Hoxton, London, aged 3 years
1866.	Jan. 18.	Elizabeth Mayhew, aged 72
	June 12.	James Walker of Wenhaston, aged 69 [M.I.]
1867.	July 2.	John Clark, aged 60 [M.I.]
	July 2.	Martha Clark of Wenhaston, aged 37 [M.I.]
	Nov. 24	Mary Tovell, aged 63
1869.	March 15.	Sarah Haward, aged 65
	June 9.	Hannah Peak of Wenhaston, aged 71 [M.I.]
1870.	Jan. 19.	Frederick Betts, aged 52 [M.I.]
	Nov. 2.	Amy Bramwell of Thorington Rectory, aged 3 years [M.I.] *Daughter of the Rector.*
1871.	March 12.	Mary Tuthill, aged 50
1872.	April 6.	Henry William Belcher of Thorington Rectory, aged 2 days [M.I.] *Child of the Rector.*
	June 11.	Harriett Mills, aged 7
	Aug. 28.	James Finch, aged 76
1873.	Jan. 16.	Hannah Howard, aged 42
	Feb. 9.	William Haylock, aged 82
	March 8.	Samuel Marshlain, aged 75 [M.I.]
	May 27.	David Mayhew of the Union House, Bulchamp, aged 83
1874.	Feb. 21.	Arthur Flatt, aged one month
	Feb. 23.	William Roberts, aged 66
	April 15	John Saker of Wenhaston, aged 41
		Lydia Saker of Wenhaston, aged 45. Husband and wife, the former died on the 8th, the latter on the 11th
	April 29.	William Fenn, aged 11 months
	Aug. 25.	Harriet Haylock, aged 28
1875.	Jan. 23.	Joseph Gilbert, aged 91
	Aug. 9.	Charles William Friend of Halesworth, aged 6 months, infant son of *the following*
	Dec. 29.	Anna Friend of Halesworth, aged 21
1876.	May 3.	Robert Cooper, aged 62. Killed by a blow on the hip from a cart-wheel
	July 13.	Samuel Gilbert, aged 25. No. 137
	Oct. 26.	Emma Flatt, aged 47. No. 138
1877.	Jan. 25.	Charles Frederick Gilbert, aged 2½ years. Only child of the above Samuel Gilbert, No. 137.
	March 10.	Charles Howard, Parish Clerk, aged 73
	March 16.	Josiah Flatt, aged 8, son of the above Emma Flatt, No. 138
1878.	May 9.	John Walker of Wenhaston, aged 85 [M.I.]

1878.	Dec. 12.	Mary Ann Howard, daughter of the Sexton, aged 20
1879.	April 6.	Walter Edward Howard, bap. March 10, 1878, aged 17 months
	July 17.	Susan Roberts, aged 20, No. 145
1880.	March 21.	Cornelius Reeve, aged 85
	May 30.	Rose Anna Roberts, aged 8, No. 147. Sister of No. 145
1881.	May 15.	Harriet Roberts, aged 15. Sister of Nos. 145, 147.
	June 3.	Henry Alexander Starkie Bence of Thorington Hall, aged 65 [M.I. *See Pedigree*]
	Sep. 17.	Emily Catling of Halesworth, aged 65 [M.I.]
1882.	Jan. 19.	Mary Eaves, aged 88

Memorial Inscriptions.

IN THE CHURCH.

MEMORIAL WINDOWS.—*The East Window.*

In memory of the Reverend THOMAS STARKIE BENCE M.A. Rector of this Parish. Born Oct. 1st 1825. Died July 14th 1858.

[*The date 1825 is an error for 1824. See his baptism.*]

The North-East Chancel Window.

In memory of Colonel HENRY BENCE BENCE. Born March 12 1788. Died Feby 9 1861.

The South-East Chancel Window.

In memory of ELIZABETH SUSANNA BENCE. Born 20th Novr 1795. Died 19th Decr 1862.

---

*On a small rectangular oblong Brass under the Altar.**

Here lyeth the Body of Robert Gould late Ministr of this Parish a faithful Teacher, both by his life and doctrine whoe departed this world ye XIth day of July 1620 aged LXII yeares.

And Jane his wife hath given this memory of him to posteritie.

*On a small stone slab under the Altar.**

Here resteth ye body of JANE daughter of FRANCIS MONKE Esqr first married to ROGER DAY Gent and after his decease to RICHARD LOVELACE of Kingsdowne in ye County of Kent Esqr whom she also overlived but had not any childe by eyther of them. She was a godly sober and vertuous woman and lived (by ye blessing of God) untill she was one hundred and eight yeares of age. In whose honour and memory Henry Coke Esqr and Margaret his wife [sole daughr and heire of ye said Richard Lovelace by Elizab his former wife] have erected this monument. This Jane for ye affectionate love she bare as well to hir husband Richard Lovelace as to the said Henry and Margret and their children gave all hir estate of Valve to those children as by hir last will appeareth. She Christianly and peacibly passed out of this mortal life ye 12 day of June 1630 in ye favour of God and good men.

* *Both of these Memorials have been removed from their original situations, and are now under the Altar, side by side, touching the East wall.*

MEMORIAL INSCRIPTIONS.   85

H
M. S.

Quicquid mortale fuit, et caducum Alex. Bence. Ar.
(Filii unici Alex. Bence. Ar. et Christianæ uxoris ejus)
Nominis haud ita pridem merito laudati.
Cui erga Parentes Pietas, erga Amicos Liberalitas,
Erga Familiares Comitas, quando ullum invenient parem.
In eo extitére quæcunq Genus
Humanum ornant, et commendant Virtutes, adeo
Ut jure dici possit, Virum fuisse
Bonum et eximium.
Sibi gratulenttur Ædes Carth. et Aul. S. Cathar
Cantab. quod in his, quæ postea ad tantum
Evexit fastigium, se Scientiæ Principiis imbuerat.
Et pari Jure Hospitium Med. Tem. Londinense.
Ubi ex operâ in Studiis Legum perquam
fæliciter impensâ, Vir tandem
Ornatissimus enituit, et præstantissimus.
Fato autem heu nimis properanti abreptus.
Spemq omnem de se haud temere conceptam
statim dissipanti.
Terrenas hasce Exuvias
Hic deposuit, Annum circa trigesimum primum
Ætatis suæ florentissimæ.
Anno autem Salutis 1742.
Sororibus, quas duas reliquit
Mutuo desideratus, flebilis occidit
Sed Neutri flebilior, quam Patri pientissimo,
Cujus, hoc lugubre Marmor, ne tantæ
Immemores forent Virtutis ingrate.
Posteri, extruendum curavit
Amor paternus.

In Eodem Tumulo
Quiescit MARIA BENCE
Una Supradict : Sororum
Obiit Anno { Ætatis 48
             Salutis 1756.

Jacent Ibidem Exuviæ
ALEXANDRI BENCE Armigeri,
Ex Antiqua Stirpe Oriundi.
Lector
Si vis Scire Vir Qualis erat ;
Justitia. Fide, et Constantia,
Eximius fuit.
Fari quæ Sensit quæ Statuit aggredi.
Promptus et Intrepidus
Gravis Idem et Cordatus.

Leges, Instituta et Sacra Majorum
Unice Dilexit ;
Patriæ Jura et Decus asseruit,
Commoda Propugnavit,
Pessum Ruituris Reipublicæ Fortunis,
Quoad Erat Privati,
(Erat autem Suffragium, Erat Auctoritas)
Diu Obnixus :
Ad ævi Melioris orientia Signa,
æquo Nimirum Aspirante Numine,
Sanus Pervixit ;
Quo tandem Omine
Spes Inter Maximas haud Evanescente,
Latior Migravit
Anno { Ætatis 88
        Salutis 1759.

Sacred to the Memory of
ANN GOLDING
sole surviving Daughter and Heiress
of ALEXANDER BENCE Esqr
late of this Place, and Wife of
GEORGE GOLDING Esqr of Poslingford
in this County
She was Buried October the 3rd 1794
Aged 80 years
In the various offices of Life, She was a dutiful Daughter and
exemplary Wife, Pious, Charitable, and Affectionate, She liv'd Beloved
and died Lamented
This Monument is erected by her Kinsman the Revnd
BENCE BENCE in Memory of her Virtues and his esteem and
Gratitude.

———

Sacred
To the Memory of
MARIANNE KATHARINE
STARKIE BENCE
Born 3rd November 1817
Died 21st May 1833.
[*She was born and baptized Nov. 2, 1817, at Kelsale in this County.*]

———

REREDOS IN MEMORY OF H. A. S. BENCE, ESQ.

The reredos is executed in Baltic and Belgian oak ; it consists of three central panels, with wings and "returns" on the sides of the chancel. The central panels consist of three cusped arches, divided by buttresses, which terminate in crocketed finials. In these arches are three subjects carved in oak, which represent the following scenes. In the centre is the group of the "Crucifixion." Our Saviour is shewn on the cross, the figures of the Blessed Virgin and of St. John stand by the sides; above their heads we see the sun and moon,—emblems of the eclipse that took place at the solemn moment of our Saviour's death. In the background is seen the city of Jerusalem. On the dexter side of the reredos is represented the scene of the "miraculous draught of fishes," and on the left side "St. Peter walking on the sea," in which the Saviour is seen standing on the sea, and raising St. Peter, who is sinking into the waves. All these groups are carved in high relief, and are beautifully executed. The style of the carving is that of the fifteenth century, of the best type. The central compartment of the reredos is surmounted by a "brattish-ing" or cresting of pierced foliage, whilst under this member is a moulding, in the hollow of which vine leaves are sunk. Between each of the three figure "panels" are four smaller ones, in which are quaintly carved the lily, passion-flower, rose, and pomegranate. The wings, as well as the sides or "returns" of the reredos, consist of framed panels of fifteenth century type. The arms of the Bence family, as well as the following inscription, " To the glory of God and in loving memory of Henry Alexander Starkie Bence, born May 15, 1816, died May 30, 1881," are carved on the upper part of the right or N. side. The antique altar table, which is of Jacobean type, is so placed as to stand in a recess, in the centre of the reredos. This table is also raised on an oak step or platform, of which the front is decorated with carved rosettes or " bosses." This altar table is covered by a richly embroidered frontal and super-frontal, on which are executed in rich colours and gold the cross keys of St. Peter and pomegranates, the grounds being in damask and velvet of antique designs. The ancient " aumbery " and piscina which have been incorporated into the design of this reredos have also been restored and decorated, and its shelf in oak has once more been replaced. The character of all the work is of the type prevalent in Suffolk in the fifteenth century.[*]

IN THE CHURCHYARD.
(*Arranged alphabetically.*)

In Memory
of
JANE the wife of
ISAAC ADAMS
Who died 1st Aug.
1811
Aged 31 years
Also of HARRIOT their
Daughter who died 5 June
1811
Aged 4 years.

In Memory of (ANNE: much respected) The Wife of
JAMES ALDIS of this Parish Farmer who Died of
Typhus Fever, on the 19th of January 1838 aged 60 years.
Immediately on the Left lie buried also Ten of their Children
six of whom, died of the same malignant Disorder; and they
were all interred within the short space of seventeen Weeks.

In
Memory of
WILLIAM son of
JAMES & ANNE ALDIS,
Who died April 22nd 1807
Aged 6 Days
Also of
Anne their daughter
Who died April 18th 1815
Aged 15 months.

[*] This work was executed by Messrs. Cox, Sons, Buckley, and Co., of London.

This Stone
is erected to perpetuate
The memory of
JAMES Eldest Son of
JAMES & ANNE ALDIS,
of this Parish,
Who was born March 23rd
1808
Departed this life Septr 7th
1831
Also in the same grave are
Interr'd ANN, their daughter
Who died Feby 7 1834
Aged 17 years.

———

In
Memory of
MARIANNE Daughter of
JAMES & ANNE ALDIS
Who died Decr 13th In
The Morning 1837
Aged 25 years
Also of
Martha their Daughter
Who died Decr 13th In the
Evening 1837
Aged 22 years.

———

In
Memory of
CAROLINE Daughter of
JAMES & ANNE ALDIS
Who died Jany 5th 1838
Aged 17 years
Also of
ELIZABETH their Daughter
Who died Feby 8th 1838
Aged 31 years.

———

In
Memory of
JOHN son of
JAMES & ANNE ALDIS
Who died Feby 18th 1838
Aged 20 years
Also of
ELIZA their Daughter
Who died April 11th 1838
Aged 19 years.

Sacred To The Memory Of
JAMES ALDIS, Farmer
Many Years Resident Of This Parish
Who Died July 18th 1843
Aged 69 years.

Sacred
To
The Memory of
AMY APPLETON
Who
Departed this life
July 20th 1844
Aged 21 years.

Sacred
To the Memory of

SUSAN wife of	ROBt APPLETON
ROBt APPLETON	Who departed
Who departed	This life
This life	August 3rd
June 12th 1861	1859
Aged 66 years.	Aged 68 years.

HARRY WILLIAM
Infant son of
the
Rev. W. BELCHER
Rector of this Parish
And EDITH his wife
died April 3, 1872.

SERVANTS IN THE BENCE FAMILY.

Here Resteth the Body of
MARGARt BISHOP, Aged 53
Who was Servt & Housekeeper in the
Family of ALEXr BENCE Esqr
24 years & after Discharging that trust
with the Strictest Fidelity & Highest
Approbation :
She departed this Life Feby 17th 1761 :
with a Joyful Expectation of receiveing
from Her Merciful REDEEMER and
JUDGE
That Gracious Eulogy of
Well Done Thou Good And
Faithful Servant.

In
Memory of
MARIA CLARK
For 18 years Housekeeper
In the Family of
Colonel BENCE.
After discharging that Trust
with the Strictest Fidelity
She departed this life
On the 16th of November
1855
Aged 66 years.

———

In
Memory of
SAMUEL MARSHLAIN
Born Feby 26th 1797
Died March 2nd 1873.
He was for 45 years a most
Faithful Servant to
Colonel BENCE and his family,
By whom this stone is placed to
Commemorate his worth and their
friendship.
[*Aged 75 years in the Burial Register.*]

———

In
Memory of
SARAH
The Wife of
SAMUEL MARSHLAIN
Who died August 6th
1846
Aged 50 years.
[*Aged 51 years in the Burial Register.*]

———

In Memory of
FREDERICK BETTS
Who died Jany 14th 1870
Aged 52 years.

———

I. H. S.
AMY
The dearly loved child
of the Rev^d A BRAMWELL
Rector of this Parish
Who died Octr 30th 1870
Aged 3 years.

In
Memory of
SARAH BREEZE
Who died
April 4th 1830
Aged 26 years.

Sacred
To the Memory of
NICHOLAS BUCKINGHAM
(Formerly of this Parish and Late
of Wenhaston)
Who departed this life in the faith
of Christ Crucified
on the 17th Day of Decr 1843
Aged 81 years.

Sacred
To the Memory of
MILDRED the wife of
NICHOLAS BUCKINGHAM
Who departed this Life in Peace
on the 5th Day of Sepr 1846
Aged 73 years.
[*Aged 74 years in the Burial Register.*]

In
Memory of
THOMAS
Son of
THO^s & MARY BURGESS
Who died Decr 21st 1821
Aged 3 years.
[*Aged 2 years in the Burial Register.*]

EMILY CATLING, sister of ANN LINES.

———   *See below*, p. 95.

In affectionate Remembrance
of
JOHN CLARKE
Who died
June 28th 1867
Aged 61 years.
[*Aged 60 years in the Burial Register.*]
Also of MARTHA
The Beloved Wife of
JABEZ CLARKE
Who died June 28th 1867
Aged 37 years.

———

Here
lies interred
the Body of
VALENTINE COATES
Who was born at
Hinton Hall
March 31st (o.s.) 1746
and died at
Thorington
Feby 29th
1818.
[*Died Saturday Feb. 28th in the Burial Register.*]

———

In Memory
of
FRANCIS DOCKING
Who died June 25th 1764
Aged 59 years.
Also
FRANCIS his Son
Aged 9 years.
[*Buried May 23rd 1754.*]

———

In
Memory of
SARAH wife of
ROBERT EDMENTS
Who departed this Life
Jany 7th 1826
Aged 42 years
[*Edmunds in the Burial Register.*]

In
Memory of
ROBERT EDMENTS
Who died
Dec. 17th 1832
Aged 64 years.

Sacred
To the Memory of
THO^s FARMELO
Who was born May 17th
1789
and departed this life
In Peace April 12th 1853.

In
Memory of
ELIZth the wife
of JOHN FIELD and
Daughter of
JAMES JAMES Who
died Novr 5, 1751
Aged 24 years.

MARY FISHER, sister of ALBAN PEAK.

See below, p. 96.

In
Memory of

MARY wife of	JAMES FRIEND
JAMES FRIEND	Who died
Who died	June 28th
May 9th 1839	1858
Aged 43 years.	Aged 80 years.

In Memory of
THO^s GIRLING
Who died 3rd March
1795
Aged 66 years.

In Memory of
SUSAN wife of
THO^s GIRLING
Who died 13th Oct^r
1796
Aged 74 years.

This Stone is erected
to perpetuate the Memory
of Eliz[th] the beloved wife
of Rich[d] Girling
Who after a long and painful
affliction peaceably resign'd her soul
into the hands of God Who gave it
July 2nd 1822 in the fortieth
year of her Age.

———

Beneath
This Tomb Resteth
In Full Hopes of
a Joyful Resurrection
The Remains of
William Girling
and Susan His Wife
(Late of Bramfield)
They lived
Universally Beloved
And Died
Deservedly Lamented
He Died Oct[r] 9th 1830
Aged 73 years.
She Died Sept[r] 23, 1828
Aged 75 years.
[*Aged 76 years in the Burial Register.*]

———

Sacred to the Memory of
Thomas Girling
Who departed this life
The 13th day of February 1855
In the 73rd year of His Age.
[*Aged 73 years in the Burial Register.*]

———

Sacred to the Memory of
Sarah the wife of Tho[s] Girling
Who departed this life
The 10th day of March 1855
In the 77th year of her age.
[*Aged 77 years in the Burial Register.*]

———

In Memory of
James James
Who died Nov[r] 30th
1772
Aged 71 years.

Sacred
To the Memory of

| SARAH wife of | WILL^m KNIGHTS |

SARAH wife of
WILL^m KNIGHTS
Who died
September 1, 1790
Aged 40 years.

WILL^m KNIGHTS
Who died
December 25
1836
Aged 85 years.

[Buried Sep. 4, 1791.   Aged 39 years, see Burial Register.]

Sacred
To the Memory of
WILLIAM LINES
Who died
13th Feb^{ry} 1803
Aged 4 years.
[Aged 3 years in the Burial Register.]

In Memory of
THOMAS LINES
Who died
18th May 1818
Aged 54 years.

In Memory of
ELIZABETH
the Wife of
THO^s LINES
Who died Novr 29th
1834
Aged 63 years.

In
Memory of
THOMAS LINES
Son of
THO^s & ELIZAth LINES
Who died Novr 9th 1841
Aged 37 years.

In Memory of
ANN LINES
Who died
Sep^{tr} 16th 1852
Aged 43 years.

On the same stone as Ann Lines.
Also of EMILY
the beloved Wife of
S. B. CATLING [of Halesworth]
and Sister of the above
Who died Sep. 14th 1881
Aged 65 years.

Here lieth the Body of
The Reverend JOHN MAYHEW
Who departed this life Sept^{er} 28, 1693
Aged 53
Here lieth the Body of
M^{rs} ANN MAYHEW
Who departed this life Sept^{er} 30, 1721
Aged 74.

Sacred
To
The Memory of
IDA AGNES
youngest daughter of
HENRY and MARIA OWLES
Who died 18th July 1865
Aged 3 years & 10 months.
Also Three Infant Sons.

In Memory of

ALBAN PEAK	MARY the wife of
son of	JAMES FISHER
W. & MARGARET PEAK	and Daughter of
died 6th July 1808	W. & MARGARET PEAK
Aged 22 years.	died 26 July 1808
	Aged 29 years.
	[*Aged 30 years in the Burial Register.*]

Sacred
To the Memory of

MARGARET wife of	WILLIAM PEAK
WILLIAM PEAK	(land Surveyor)
Who died	Who died
Novr 19th 1828	6th Feby 1810
Aged 83 years.	Aged 66 years.

Sacred
To the Memory of
JAMES the son of
JAMES and HANNAH PEAK
Who died April 27th 1832
Aged 1 year
and 11 months.
[*Entered in the Register as Robert James Peak.*]

———

In Memory of
JAMES PEAK
Who died November 16th 1862
Aged 73 years.
Also of
HANNAH the wife of
JAMES PEAK
Who died June 4th 1869
Aged 72 years.
[*Aged 71 years in the Burial Register.*]

———

In
Memory of
CHARLES CLODE
Row
Who died June 26th
1856
Aged 2 years & 3 months.

———

In Memory of
JAMES son of
JAMES & SARAH RUSH
Late of this Parish
Who died Decr 24th
1853
Aged 13 years.

———

In Memory of
PHILIP STROWGER
Who died
5th July 1804
Aged 68 years.

o

In Memory of
MARTHA wife of
PHILIP STROWGER
Who died
Aug. 17th 1831
Aged 94 years.

Sacred
To the Memory of

MARGARET WALKER wife of THO' WALKER Who died Sep^{tr} 21st 1842 Aged 73 years. [*Aged 71 years in the Burial Register.*]	THOMAS WALKER Who died 27th Octr 1818 Aged 66 years. [*Aged 65 years in the Burial Register.*]

In Memory of
HANNAH WALKER
Who died March 12
1854
Aged 54 years.
[*Aged 55 years in the Burial Register.*]

In Memory of
MARY WALKER
Who died
January 11th 1865
Aged 62 years.

In Memory of
JAMES WALKER
Who died
June 9th 1866
Aged 69 years.

In Memory of
JOHN WALKER
Late of Wissett
Died May 5th 1878
Aged 85 years.

NOTICES OF MONUMENTAL INSCRIPTIONS IN DAVY'S MSS., 1806.

FOL. 392, 394.

In the Chancel.

1. Against the east end and on the north side is a mural monument of white marble, being a plain square tablet, surmounted by a triangular pediment, and over it a circular urn and two antique lamps. On the tablet this inscription :

Inscription to Alexander Bence, 1742. (*See page* 85.)

Below this, on another tablet, which appears to have been since added, is the following :

Inscriptions to Mary Bence, 1756, *and Alexander Bence,* 1759. (*See page* 85.)

Arms below : Bence, with a label of three points. Crest of Bence.

2. On the south side of the east window is a plain black marble tablet standing on a plain cornice.

Inscription to Jane Lovelace. (*See page* 84.)

The arms below were of eight coats. The first appears to have been Coke, and the fourth Sa. a chevron between three covered cups or. The other coats are not to be distinguished.

On the moulding of the cornice below :

At the feet of the said Jane Lovelace lye buried y⁰ bodies of Robert and Thomas Coke sons of yᵉ abovesaid Henry and Margaret. Robert dyed 20 Dec. 1630. Thomas dyed 18 Apr. 1631, both infants.

3. On a flat stone within the Communion rails is a brass plate, above which was a shield of arms, or group of children, on brass also, now gone. With the following inscription :

Inscription to Robert Golde. (*See page* 84.)

4. In the middle of the chancel, on a small brass plate, in black letter :

Xp'e Jh'u vere
Roberti Wode
Miserere.

This had disappeared in 1813.

FOL. 394.

Mr. Bouett's hand [of Griston, Norf.], Blomef., vol. i., p. 572.

Thorington.

Monument, No. 2. Arms at top in a lozenge.

Monke—Gu. a chevron arg. betwn. 3 lions' heads erased of 2nd.

Just below this, and immediately above the tablet, 3 coats.

Dexter—1. Day. Erm. on a chief indented az. 2 eaglets displd. arg., impaling Monke.

Sinister—2. Lovelace. Quarterly—1 and 4. Gu. on a chief indented sa. 3 martlets arg. 2 and 3. Az. on a saltire arg. 5 martlets sa.

Centre—3. Lovelace, Day and Monke impaled.

Below :

Coke.   Quarterly.—1. Coke p. pale gu. and az. 3 eagles displayed arg.

            2. Arg. a chevron between 3 chaplets gu.

            3. Sa. a chevron or between 3 cups covered of the 2nd.

            4. Gu. a griffin rampant or between 7 cross-crosslets
               fitchee of 2nd.

        Impaling Lovelace.

Fol. 305.   FURTHER CHURCH NOTES TAKEN MAY 21, 1830.   (No. 79.)

Lovelace's monument, which was formerly fixed against the east wall of the chancel on the south side, has been taken down, and the tablet only, of black marble, preserved, which is laid in the floor just below ; the inscription, never intended for the rough use it will now occasionally be put to, cannot last a very long time.   Inscription below and arms gone.

The stone for Rob. Gould lies north and south against the east wall of the chancel, towards the north side.

The monument for Alexander Bence has been removed from the east end, north side of the window, to the north wall, about the centre of the chancel, and is not otherwise altered.

Mrs. Golding's monument, which is against the north wall of the nave, I find I have noticed.

(*After a few more lines, he notes the monument and gives the inscriptions as above.*)

REGISTERS OF THE FAMILY ÓF BENCE.

ALDEBURGII.
Baptisms.

1560.	May 5.	Margett daughter of John Bence
	.... 19.	Joane daughter of Edmond Bens
1561.	Aug. 24.	Edmond son of Edmoud Bens
1563.	Aug. 29.	Thomas son of Edmond Bens
1564.	Sep. 17.	Rose daughter of Edmond Bens
1565.	Dec. 26.	Ales daughter of Edmond Bens and Margerie his wife
1567.	July 20.	Rose daughter of Edmond Bense and Margerie his wife
1568.	May 28.	Eme daughter of John Bense and Joane his wife
1570.	Nov. 2.	Robert son of Edmond Bense and Margerie his wife
1573.	April 26.	John son of Edmond Bence and Margerie his wife
1574.	Dec. 21.	Thomas son of Alexander Bence and Marie his wife
1576.	Aug. 12.	Joane daughter of Robert Bence jun. and Bridget his wife
	Aug. 26.	John son of William Bence and Marie his wife
1577.	July 28.	Alexander son of Alexander Bence and Marie his wife
1578.	Aug. 10.	William son of William Bence and Marie his wife
	Sep. 28.	John son of Robert Bence and Bridget his wife
1579.	Nov. 29.	Margaret daughter of Robert Bence and Bridget his wife
1581.	April 30.	John son of Alexander Bence and Marie his wife
	Oct. 1.	Robert son of William Bence and Marie his wife
1583.	June 9.	Rose daughter of Edmond Bence the elder and Joane his wife
1584.	Jan. 12.	Marye daughter of William Bence and Marie his wife
1584.	Feb. 28.	Robert son of Alexander Bence and Marie his wife
1587.	July 16.	John son of William Bence and Marie his wife
	Oct. 16.	William son of Alexander Bence and Marie his wife
1591.	Dec. 5.	William son of Alexander Bence and Marie his wife
1594.	June 23.	Alexander son of Alexander Bence the younger and Marie his wife
1597.	April 17.	Squier son of ....
		Marie daughter of Alexander Bence the younger and Marie his wife

Marriages.

1565.	Jan. 6.	Robert Burgis and Marget Bense
1571.	June 25.	Thomas Benze and Isabel Lambe widow
	Sep. 2.	Alexander Bence and Marie Squier
1574.	Aug. 29.	Arthur Michelson and Joane daughter of John Bence
	Oct. 25.	Robert Bence sen. and Anne Willett
1575.	April 10.	William Bence and Mary Wright widow
	May 18.	Edmond Page and Margaret daughter of Edmund Bence the elder
	June 13.	Edmund Bence the younger and Elizabeth Cressey widow

1575. Aug. 29.   Robert Bence jun. and Bridget Coverdale
1580. Sep. 4.   William Hales and Margerie Bence
1588. Aug. 26.   William Browse and Joane Bence both single
1590. Dec. 15.   Robert Dymor and Rose Bence both single
1591. Aug. 22.   Richard Atkinson and Rose Bence both single
1597. Sep. 24.   Edmund Bence widower and Bridget Chaney widow
1600. July 11.   Alexander Bence jun. and Rose Johnson both single

Burials.

1558. March 10.   Margaret Bence widow
      March 25.   Margaret daughter of John Bence
1568. June 6.   Eme daughter of John Bense and Joane his wife
1570. Sep. 7.   John son of John Bence and Joane his wife
1573. Aug. 31.   Ales daughter of Edmond Bence and Margerie his wife
1574. March 28.   Ales wife of Robert Bence
1577. March 27.   John Bence
1578. Nov. 20.   John son of William Bence and Marie his wife
1583. Aug. 18.   Rose daughter of Edmond Bence the elder and Joane his wife
1585. March 10.   Joane Bence widow
1587. Dec. 10.   William son of Alexander Bence
158¼. Feb. 10.   Robert Bence the elder
1591. Nov. 23.   Lewis son of John Bence and Agnes his wife
1597. May 27.   William son of Alexander Bence
      June 20.   Elizabeth wife of Edmond Bence
159¼. March 11.   Edmond Bence who was some time bailiff

BECCLES.

Baptisms.

1787. April 28.   Anna Maria daughter of Bence Sparrow [afterwards Bence]
                  and Harriet his wife
1788. March 12.   Henry Bence son of the same
1791. March 5.   Matilda daughter of the same

Marriages.

1786. May 16.   Bence Sparrow, Rector of the parish, and Harriet Elmy both
                  single
1811. July 17.   William Jones, Lieut.-Col. 5th Dragoon Guards, and Matilda
                  Bence
1812. March 17.   Rev. Lancelot Robert Brown and Anna Maria Bence

BENHALL.

Baptisms.

1670. Sep. 27.   John son of Edmund Bence and Mary his wife
1671. Feb. 20.   Alexander son of the same
1673. May 25.   Edmund son of the same
1675. Jan. 23.   Mary daughter of the same
1677. July 5.   Edmund son of the same
1678. Oct. 6.   William son of the same
1679. Jan. 20.   Thomas son of the same
1681. Aug. 5.   Abigail daughter of the same

Burials.

1678.	Oct. 10.	William son of Edmund Bence
	Oct. 23.	Edmund son of Edmund Bence
1683.	Sep. 15.	Ann Bence
1702.	May 7.	Edmund Bence
1717.	May 15.	Mary Bence
1751.	March 25.	Mrs. Abigail Bence of Saxmundham
1765.	Jan. 25.	Mary Bence

CARLETON.

Marriage.

1747.	Sep. 30.	Mr. Gabriel Trusson and Mrs. Katharine Bence [both single] of Kelsale

Burials.

1712.	June 5.	Edmund son of Thomas and Margaret Bence
1737.	Oct. 11.	Mrs. Margaret Bence wife of Rev. Mr. Thomas Bence
1757.	Sep. 27.	Rev. Mr. Thomas Bence, Rector of Kelsale and this parish upwards of 53 years

HENSTEAD.

Marriage.

1740.	Dec. 16.	Robert Sparrow of Kettleburgh and Anne Bence

Burials.

1745.	Dec. 22.	Robert Bence
1747.	April 2.	Lawrence Bence his son s.p.
1765.	Oct. 20.	Robert Sparrow
1776.	Nov. 16.	Mrs. Sparrow daughter of Robert Bence.
1792.	Dec. 20.	Mary Bence her sister, a maiden lady

KELSALE.

Baptisms.

1708.	Sep. 23.	Catherine daughter of Thomas and Margaret Bence
170$\frac{9}{10}$.	March 8.	Bridgett daughter of the same
1712.	May 2.	Edmund son of the same
1749.	Feb. 14.	Katherine daughter of Gabriel and Katherine Trusson
1752.	July 1.	Thomas son of the same
1817.	. . . .	Marianne Katharine Starkie daughter of Henry Bence Bence and Elizabeth Susanna his wife

Marriages.

1758.	April 28.	Thomas Bigsby of Saxmundham, Doctor of Physic, and Bridgett Bence
1769.	Feb. 21.	Anthony Collett of Walton, co. Suffolk, and Catharine Trusson both single
1815.	May 5.	Henry Bence Bence and Elizabeth Susanna Starkie both single

Burials.

1766.	June 23.	Gabriel Trusson
1785.	June 18.	Catherine relict of the late Gabriel Trusson
1868.	Feb. 18.	Rev. Lancelot Robert Brown
1872.	March 23.	Anna Maria Brown

St. Bennet Gracechurch, London.

Baptisms.

1653.	Feb. 8.	Alexander son of Robert Bence and Elizabeth his wife
1656.	March 27.	Jacob son of Robert Bence, deceased, and Elizabeth his wife

Burials.

1654.	Aug. 31.	Alexander son of Robert Bence
1655.	March 20.	Robert Bence
1696.	Feb. 10.	Elizabeth Bence

St. Dunstan in the East, London.

Burial.

1611.	June 4.	Robert Bence of Harwich

St. Mary at Hill, London.

Burial.

1590.	May 16.	Thomas Bence

Sibton.

Baptisms.

1706.	Oct. 8.	Laurence son of Robert Bence and Mary his wife
170¾.	Jan. 31.	Anne daughter of the same
1709.	Sept. 30.	Mary daughter of the same

Burial.

1717.	Aug. 27.	Mary* wife of Robert Bence obiit 24° 3tiâ horâ matutinâ

Westleton.

Baptisms.

1625.	Sep. 6.	Elizabeth daughter of John Bence
1629.	Sep. 9.	John son of John Bence
1631.	Jan. 7.	William son of John Bence and Priscilla his wife
1653.	Dec. 21.	Joyce daughter of William Bence and Mary his wife
1655.	April 12.	William son of the same
1656.	Nov. 7.	John son of the same

Marriage.

1686.	Dec. 9.	John Snell of Chediston and Mistress Priscilla Bence of Halesworth both single

Burials.

1624.	June 18.	Joyce daughter of John Bence
1633.	Oct. 8.	John Bence
1655.	April 12.	William son of William Bence and Mary his wife
1670.	Nov. 2.	Widd. Bence [Priscilla]

---

* In the Bence Pedigree she is said to be buried at Henstead, a mistake I was not aware of till I saw this register of her burial at Sibton, and her altar-tomb in the churchyard.—T. S. H.

MONUMENTAL INSCRIPTIONS

OF THE

FAMILY OF BENCE.

ALDEBURGH.

On a brass on a flat stone at the east end of the South Chancel Aisle.

HIC IACET GVILIELMVS BENCE DVM VIXIT VNVS
CAPITLI'V BVRGESIVM ISTIVS VILLE QVI OBIJT SECVN
DO DIE SEPTEMBRIS ANNO D'NI 1606 AN'OQ' ÆTATIS
SVE 57 ET NVPTVS MARIÆ BLOME RELIQVIT PLES
ROB'TVM, IOH'EM, THOMAM, ET MARIAM, EXPECTANS
RESVRRECC'OEM MORTVORVM.

Below this inscription is a male figure in bailiff's gown and ruff collar, and a female figure in hat and ruff collar, followed by the ensuing lines:

IF TO BE IVST, RELIGIOVS, WISE, AND FREE
HE MANS : OR HIS, WHAT BETTER COVLD THERE BEE
TO STRAVNGERS KINDE, AND TO HIS HOME SO DEARE
WELL KNOWNE FOR TRAFFICK, WTH THOSE NATIONS NEARE
IF TO ATTAINE A COMPETENT POSSESSION
BY FAITHFVLL PAINES FREED FROM OPPRESSION
OR OF HIS WORD SO CIRCVMSPECT AND SOVNDE
AS THAT THE SAME BEYOND THE LAWES HIM BOVNDE
AND BY THAT STRAIGHT RVLE W^{CH} EXPERIENCE BRINGS
TOOKE THE TRVE HEIGHT OF MOMENTARY THINGS
BOLDLY HER BENCE MAY ALDBOROVGH PREFERRE
WHOME AS SHE BREDD HERE KINDELY DOTH INTERR.

By the side of the above.

HERE LYETH BVRIED THE BODY OF ALEXANDER THE SONNE OF IOHN
BENCE, WHO HAD TO WIFE MARY Y^E DAVGHTER OF THOMAS SQVIER,
THEY LIVED TOGEATHER 38 YEARES & 4 MONETHES . AND HAD ISSVE
9 SONNES & 2 DAVGHTERS, WHEREOF ARE LIVINGE IOHN, ROBERT,
ALEX^R & SQVIER . ROSSE & MARY, HE WAS BAILIFFE OF THIS CORPORATIO'
SIX TIMES . HE DECEASED THE 27TH OF IANVARY . 1612 . ÆTATIS SVÆ 65.

Above this inscription is a male figure in bailiff's gown and ruff collar. The wife's figure is missing, as also a shield above the figures bearing a ship—the arms of Aldborough.
Below the inscription, nine sons on left; two daughters on right, on one brass plate.

P

Formerly in Chancel.

*Male figure in bailiff's gown and ruff collar between two wives in ruffe collars
and hats.*

HERE LYETH BVRIED THE BODY OF IOHN THE SON OF
ALEXANDER BENCE WHO HAD TWO WIVES MARY AND
ELIZABETH BY HIS FIRST WIFE MARY WHO LYETH INTER-
RED BY HIM HE HAD ISSVE 4 SON'ES & TWO DAVGHTERS, VIZ.
IOHN ALEXANDER EDMVND MARY AND ELIZABET THESE FIVE
WEARE LIVING AT HIS DEATH, HE WAS BAYLIF OF THIS COR-
PORATION FOVER TIMES, AND DYED THE SECOND OF IVLY
ANNO DOMINI 1635 ÆTATIS SVÆ 54.

Below, a small brass with four sons, and another with two daughters.

Copies of these brasses and inscriptions were taken some years ago, probably
between thirty and forty, but the date is uncertain.   Of these the first was described
as being on a flat stone in the middle of the church ; it is now at the east end of
the south chancel aisle, and is perfect.   The second, now by the side of the former,
was then in the chancel.   The shield of arms and figure of the wife were then
existing.   The third inscription was described at that time as being in the chancel,
but now no trace of figure or inscription can be found.   Rubbings of these brasses
as they were then are in the possession of Captain Starkie Bence of Kentwell
Hall, Suffolk.

Churchyard.

Mrs Mary Bence Widow of Squier Bence died 24 October 1678.

Here lyeth the Body of Squier Bence the son of Alexander Bence.   He had
two wives, Elizabeth and Mary.   By his first had two children, who died young
was Bailiff three times and Burgess in Parliament twice.   Died 27 November
1648 aged 51 years 6 months and twelve days.

These inscriptions are not now to be found.

BECCLES.

Chancel.

Sacred to the Memory of Harriot the much lamented wife of the Revnd B.
Bence Rector of this Parish and Daughter of William Elmy Esq. and of Catharine
Pullen his wife.   She died June the 9th 1815.   Aged 56 years.

Also in Memory of the above named Bence Bence a faithful teacher of God's
word both by his Life and Doctrine.   He departed this life the 2nd of Septr 1824,
aged 77 years.*

A Monumental Inscription to William Elmy, Esq., who died June 9, 1801, aged
86 years ; and to Catharine his widow, daughter of Peter Pullyn, Esq., who died
March 22, 1808, aged 80 years.   And to other members of the Elmy family.

Also, on the north wall, within the altar rails, a memorial of Katharine widow
of Nicholas Starkie, Esq., of Frenchwood in Lancashire, and youngest daughter of
Robert Edgar, Esq., of Ipswich.   She died April 10, 1814, in the 47th year of her
age, leaving two daughters.

* At the restoration of Beccles Church the flat stone covering the grave of Bence Bence and
his wife was removed from the chancel to the nave.

BENHALL.

Church.

Hic jacet Edmundus Bence Armiger Obijt quinto die Maij Anno Ætatis suæ 83 Anno Dom. 1702. A parte sinistra viri sui Positum est quod mortale Mariæ Bence vitam dum Egit providam multæ Consulens Proli vicinis Chara Pauperibus Munifica Animam reddidit Maij 10 Ætatis 69, anno 1717.

Here lieth the Body of Mary Bence daughter of Edmund and Mary Bence late of this Parish who departed this life the 16th Jan'y 1765 aged 93. And Abigail daughter of the said Edmund and Mary Bence who departed this life the 10th March 1750 aged 68.

CARLTON.

Churchyard.

Hic manent in Tumulo Corpuscula Thomæ Bence A.M. plus quam 50 Annos hujus Ecclesiæ Recto' humili spe Resurrectionis Carnis et Vitæ æternæ obiit vicesimo primo Septembris 1757.

Et Margarettæ Uxoris ejus Filiæ Roberti Barker de Bredfield in hoc Comitatu Armigeri obiit Illa tertio Octobris 1737.

Et Edmundi Bence filii Dictorum Obiit Junii tertio Circiter unius mensis Ætatis.

In Memory of Bridgett Bigsby the Beloved wife of Thomas Bigsby, M.D., and Daughter of the Rev. Mr Tho. Bence, A.M., who died 7th May 1772, aged 63.

HENSTEAD.

Panel of four.

Robert the 3rd son of Edmund Bence of Benhall died Dec. 19th 1745 aged 72 years.

Robert Sparrow of Worlingham died Sept. 15th 1765 aged 60 years.

Anne wife of Robert Sparrow and daughter of Robert Bence died Nov. 8th 1776 aged 68 years.

Laurence the only son of Robert and Mary Bence daughter of Laurence Eachard A.M. died March 31st 1747 aged 41 years.

Chancel.

In grateful and affectionate regard this monument is erected to Mary Bence second Daughter of Robert Bence formerly of this Parish whose remains together rest in the Vault at the west end of this Church. Thro' a long life she performed every Duty within her sphere and died deeply lamented Dec. 21, 1792, aged 83 years.

Churchyard.

In hopes of a joyful Resurrection here rest the Bodies of Robert Bence and Lawrence Bence his son both of this Parish, Gentlemen. Robert died and buried 19th Dec. 1745, aged 72 years. Lawrence on the 31st March 1746, aged 41.

HEVENINGHAM.

Chancel.

Here lyeth ye Body of Katherine the wife of John Bence of Heveningham,

Esq., daughter of Sr Sackville Glemham, of Glemham in this County, who departed this life March 1st 1715.

Here lyeth the Body of John Bence Esq. who departed this life the 18th of October 1718, aged 48 years.

KELSALE.

Church.

Sacred to the memory of the Rev. Lancelot Robert Brown who departed this life Feb. 11, 1868, aged 82 years. He was Rector of this Parish and Carlton for 58 years.

Also of Anna Maria Relict of the above who departed this life March 17th, 1872, aged 85 years.

Churchyard.

To the memory of Gabriel Trusson Esq. who died 17 June 1766, aged 54, and of Catharine his wife Eldest Daughter of the Rev. Thomas Bence Rector of this Parish, who died 8 June 1785, aged 77.

SIBTON.

Churchyard.

In hope of a joyful Resurrection
Here lyeth the Body of Mrs Mary
Bence wife of Mr Robert Bence
of Henstead in this County who depart^d
this life on the 21 (?) Day of August
1717.   Aged 33 (?) years.

Erected by A. Sparrow and M. Bence, her Daughters.

APPENDIX.

————◆————

REGISTERS OF BAPTISMS, MARRIAGES, AND BURIALS THAT
HAVE TAKEN PLACE AT THORINGTON SINCE 1881, AFTER
THE FORMER PAGES WERE PRINTED.

Baptisms.

1882.	April 2.	Richard Alexander [born Jan. 29] son of Percy Bence-Trower, Esq., of 7 Stanhope Street, Hyde Park Gardens, London, and Agnes Marian [late Bence]
	April 9, Easter Day.	Chester [born Dec. 30, 1881] son of Edgar Catchpole, labouring man, and Julia [late Miles]
	May 14.	Arthur [born April 16] son of George Abel Edwards, gardener, and Emma [late Sully]
	May 28, Whit Sunday.	Emma [born April 15] daughter of John Haylock, labourer, and Harriet [late Canham]
	July 2.	George William [born May 9] son of George Mills, gardener, and Jane [late Flatt]
1883.	Jan. 28:	Sam [born Dec. 25, 1882] son of John Fenn, gamekeeper, and Susan [late Haylock]
	July 1.	Hilda Elizabeth [born Sept. 17, 1882] daughter of Frank Robert Howells, shopman, of 17 Priory Street, Camden Town, London, and Emily
	Aug. 5.	Samuel James [born April 14, 1881] son of Albert Haward, bricklayer, of 26 Bramford Road, Ipswich, and Elizabeth [late Eade]
	. . . .	Ernest Henry [born Aug. 31, 1882] son of the same
	Sept. 9.	Charles Alfred [born July 10] son of Edgar Catchpole, labouring man, and Julia [late Miles]
1884.	Jan. 27.	Edith Muriel [born Oct. 31, 1883] daughter of Percy Bence-Trower, Esq., of 7 Stanhope Street, Hyde Park Gardens, London, and Agnes Marian [late Bence]
	April 13, Easter Day.	Arthur [born Feb. 12] son of George Mayhew, labouring man, of Wenhaston, and Rachel [late Roberts]

Marriages.

1882.	Nov. 4.	Alfred Hall, 20, and Alice Flatt, 17, both single
1883.	Dec. 6.	Robert Gibbs, 24, and Mary Ann Sully, 24, both single
1884.	Jan. 23.	Guy Lenox Lambert, 27, of Brook Hill, Crossboyne, co. Mayo, Ireland, and Ida Millicent Bence, 23, both single

Burials.

1883.	Feb. 15.	Betsy Geater of Wenhaston, aged 61
	Aug. 12.	John Saker, aged 78

INDEX.

D

Dade, Thomas, 56.
Dale, Sarah, 40. 41.
Dalliman. John, 54.
Darby, Edward, 31, 75 ; Eliz., 75 ; Mary, 31.
Dashwood, George, 59 n.
Davy. Martha, 66.
Dawson, Ellen, 70 ; Robert, 15.
Day [Daye, Deye], Eliz., 15 ; Henry. 15, 17 ; Katharine, 15 ; Maryan, 15 ; Roger, 84 ; Thomas, 64.
Deaves [Deanes, Denes]. Eliz., 26, 28 ; John, 26, 28 ; Robert, 20 ; Thomas, 28.
Debenham, Andrew, 24 ; Ann, 24 ; Ellen, 24.
De Bosco, John, 29 n.; Roger. 29 n.
Denny, Anthony. 28 n.; Henry, 28 n.; Joane, 19 ; John, 19, 61 ; Margery, 19, 21 ; Matthew, 19.
Derrowe, —, 21.
Dew. Dorothy, 55.
Dinnington, Eliz., 24 ; Thomas, 24.
Ditcher. John, 63, 64.
Dix, Mary Ann, 65.
Dobbies, John. 17.
Docking [Doking], Eliz.. 33, 63 ; Francis, 33, 54, 76, 92 ; John, 33, 76 ; Sarah, 33, 76.
Donnet, Anthony, 19, 52, 69 ; Bridget, 19 ; Eliz., 19, 69 ; Em'e. 17 ; Henry, 19 ; Joane, 17, 18, 19, 20 ; Robert, 17, 18, 19, 20 ; William, 18.
Dorkins, Francis, 77.
Downing, Eliz., 61 ; Robert, 54.
Dowsine, Alice, 16.
Dowtie [Douty], Hammond, 26 ; Jane, 18 ; Margaret, 26 ; Robert, 17, 18 ; —, 26.
Drane, James, 55.
Dreane. Hannah, 54.
Drew. Eleanor, 48 ; Henry, 48, 67.
Driver, Eliz., 52, 54 ; Sarah, 43, 65 ; Susan, 55.
Drwery, Robert, 15.
Duckett. Margaret, 26 ; Nathaniel, 26 ; Theophylab, 26.
Dulfield, William, 54.
Dunne. Mr., 20.
Dunnet. Ann, 39 ; George, 39.
Dunthorn, Susan, 55.
Durrant [Durante, Durant, Dorant, Dorente, Dorent, Durrente]. Alexander. 28 ; Anes, 28 ; Ann, 26 ; Edmond, 27, 73 ; John, 26, 27, 28, 72, 73 ; Margaret, 27, 28, 74 ; Mary, 27, 28, 73 ; Mercy, 27, 55 ; Robert, 73 ; Sarah, 65 ; Susan, 73.
Dymer, Robert, 54.
Dymor, Robert, 102.

E

Eachard, Mary. 107 ; Laurence. 107.
Eade, Caroline, 50, 51, 67 ; Eliz., 51, 67, 109 ; Sarah, 67.
Eastaugh [Estaugh, Esthaugh], Abraham, 39 ; Joseph, 39 ; Margaret, 31, 32 ; Robert, 32 ; Sarah, 39, 61 ; William, 31, 32.
Eaves, Mary, 83 ; Mary Ann, 66.
Edgar. Katharine, 106 ; Robert, 106.
Edments [Edmunds], Ann, 47 ; Eliz., 43 ; Emily, 47 ; Harvey, 47 ; James, 41, 47 ; Robert, 41, 42, 43, 47, 65, 80, 92, 93 ; Samuel, 42 ; Sarah, 41, 42, 43, 47, 80, 92.

Edwards, Arthur, 109 ; Emma, 109 ; George Abel, 109 ; John, 55 ; Richard, 43 ; Rose, 58 ; Samuel, 43, 61, 65 ; Sarah, 43, 66 ; Susan, 40.
Ellet, John, 52.
Elliot. Margaret, 61.
Ellis [Ellys], Arthur, 21 ; Eliz., 55 ; Hannah, 65 ; Joane, 72 ; Margaret, 54 ; Mary, 31 ; William, 31.
Elmy. Ann, 35, 78 ; Catharine, 106 ; Emma, 51 ; George, 51 ; Harriet, 102, 106 ; Lætitia, 36 ; Louisa, 51 ; Lydia, 35, 78 ; Margaret, 35 ; Mary, 35 ; Robert, 36, 77 ; Samuel, 35, 36, 63, 77, 78, 79 ; Sarah, 35, 36, 77, 78, 79 ; Susannah. 36 ; William, 106.
Elsden, Catharine, 60 n.
Elvine. John, 70.
Emans, Dyonys. 22, 70 ; Eliz., 70 ; George, 22, 70 ; Jane. 22 ; Olyver, 22 ; Robert, 22 ; William, 22.
Engall, Eliz., 61 ; William. 64.
Esther, Judah, 33 ; Nathl., 33 ; Rebecca, 33.
Etheridge, Sarah, 46, 47, 48 ; William, 65.
Evans. Batinia, 53 ; Benjamin, 29 ; George, 29, 74 ; John, 29, 74 ; Matthew [female], 29, 74 ; Rebecca. 53, 74 ; William, 53 n., 74 n. [The above Bathia is registered as Ecan, but as she marries a "Priest" she is evidently a daughter of William Evans, the Rector.]
Everard [Evered]. Henry, 20 ; John, 20 ; Margaret, 19. 20, 71 ; Mary, 53 ; Nicholas, 19, 20, 21 ; William, 19, 20.
Everson. Mary Ann, 67.
Ewen [Ewin]. Eliz., 58 ; Nicholas, 57, 75 ; Robert, 75.

F

Farmelo, Thomas. 66, 81, 93.
Farrare, Anne, 16 ; John, 16 ; Robert, 15.
Farrow, Gabriel, 55.
Fawether. Sam., 26.
Fella, Alice, 72 ; Mary, 74 ; Matthew [female], 29 ; Robert, 29, 72 ; Susannah, 29 ; Thomas, 60, 60 n.
Felloe [Fellow, Fellowe], Alice. 24 ; Christian, 18, 20, 21, 70 ; Dorothy, 18 ; Edward, 18, 20, 21 ; Em'e. 18 ; Jason, 21 ; Joane, 19 ; Mary, 27 ; Matha, 27 ; Robert, 20, 24, 27, 53, 73.
Feltham [Feltame, Felthame], Edmund, 24, 24 n., 74 ; Harborne, 24, 25, 71, 72 ; Margaret, 24 n., 25 ; Mary, 24, 24 n., 71 ; Muriel, 24, 25, 71 ; Thomas, 24, 24 n., 71.
Fenn, John, 49, 50, 51, 67, 109 ; Kerenhappuch, 51 ; Neailly, 50 ; Robert, 51 ; Sam., 109 ; Susan, 49, 50, 51, 109 ; William, 50, 82.
Fenninge, William, 20.
Feveryear [Fevareyeare]. Alice, 17 ; Katharine, 20 ; Mary, 19 ; Rebecca, 21 ; Margery, 52.
Field, Eliz., 58, 76, 93 ; John, 61, 93.
Finch, Ann, 37, 38, 39, 41, 78, 80, 81 ; Anne Maria. 47 ; Benjamin, 37, 41, 42, 46 ; Charlotte, 37, 78 ; Eliz., 45 ; Heley. 39 ; J., 78 ; James, 37, 38, 39, 41, 45, 46, 47, 64. 66, 78, 80, 82 ; John, 41, 46 ; Lina. 45, 81 ; Mary, 41, 42 ; Phyllis, 39, 45, 66 ; Rose, 39 ; Sarah, 37, 41, 46, 65 ; Sophia, 38 ; Susan, 45, 46, 47, 81 ; William, 47.
Fisher. James. 65, 96 ; Marianne. 42, 43 ; Mary, 79, 93, 96 ; Susan. 42, 43, 44, 45, 46, 65.

37 ; Tabitha, 42, 46, 51, 81 ; William, 36, 37, 38, 39, 42, 46, 50, 64, 79, 82.
Haytbord, Timothy, 53.
Head, Joseph, 76.
Hedde, Anne. 16 ; Eliz., 16 : Freseworth, 16 ; Robert, 16.
Hensby, Faith, 66.
Herne, Mary, 54.
Heron, Henry, 59 n.
Heveningham, Henry, 59 n.
Higgins, Mary, 58.
Higaam, Thomas, 66.
Hill, George, 15.
Hilling, John, 54.
Hitcham [Hicham], Eliz., 34, 77 ; Joseph, 35 ; Mary, 35 ; Robert, 34, 35, 64, 77.
Holden, James, 66.
Honner, Eliz., 27 ; William, 27.
Horn, Ann, 38, 39, 40, 41.
Houett, Mary, 53.
Houldage, John, 24.
Houlseby, Alice, 21 : Jane, 17 ; John, 19.
How, Margaret, 30 : William, 30.
Howard, Anna, 67 ; Charles, 44, 65, 82 : Emily, 51 ; Hannah, 82 ; Mary Ann, 83; Sarah, 44 ; Walter Edward, 51, 83 ; William, 44, 66.
Howells, Emily, 109 ; Frank Robert, 109 ; Hilda Elizabeth, 109.
Howe's, Mary, 60.
Howlett, George, 65 ; Mary, 47, 48.
Hubbard, Annes, 54.
Hudson, Joseph, 53.
Huffet [Hufflet], Ann, 43, 44, 45.
Hugman, Mary, 57.
Hunebell, Eliz., 67.
Hurling, John, 55.
Hurren, Alice, 50 ; Archer, 50 ; Jane, 50 ; William, 50.
Hurriu, Richard, 61.
Hutton, Margaret, 16.

I

Ingram, Marrible, 17 ; Martha, 17 ; Thomas, 17.

J

Jackson, Mary, 75 ; Robert, 75 ; Thomas, 58.
Jaeman, Mary, 44 ; Mary Girling, 44 ; Thomas, 44.
James, Eliz., 61, 77, 93 ; James, 77, 93, 94.
Jarvis [Jarvice, Jarves], Christopher, 32, 33, 60, 77 ; Mary, 32 ; Robert, 32 ; Sarah, 32, 33, 36, 63, 76, 77, 78.
Jeffery, John, 54.
Jenkenson, Eleanor, 57.
Jermy, Amy, 63.
Jesoppe, Grace, 53.
Jessup, Martha, 62.
Jex, Hugo, 31 ; John, 31.
Johnson [Johnsone], Alice, 23 ; Ann, 22, 52 ; Bridget, 22 ; Dorothie, 69 ; Eliz., 22, 23, 69 ; Margaret, 53 ; Mary, 22 ; Rose, 102 ; Thomas, 22, 23, 52, 69, 69 n., 70 n.
Jones, Henry Bruce, 42 ; Matilda, 42 ; William, 42, 102.
Joyner, Thomas, 53.
Julians, Anthony, 55 ; John, 58 ; Joseph, 58.

K

Keeble, Richard, 57.
Kemp, Charles, 34.
Kerridge, George, 67.
Kersey, Mary, 45, 46.
Kettle, Eliz., 61.
Keyrison, John, 53.
Kinge [King], Andrew, 54 ; Ann, 23 ; Margaret, 23 ; Nicholas, 23, 52.
Knapp, James, 58 n. ; Mary, 58 n.
Knights, Ann, 36, 40, 41, 42, 43, 44, 65 ; Ellen, 49 ; George, 49, 67, 82 ; John, 66 ; Mary, 37, 62, 63 ; Mary Ann, 49 ; Mary Anna, 49 ; Richard, 36, 77 ; Robert, 54 ; Sarah, 36, 37, 64, 77, 78, 95 ; William, 36, 37, 77, 78, 80, 95.
Knoller, Eliz., 33 ; John, 33 ; Judah, 76 ; William, 33.
Kynnaston, Francis, 24.

L

Lamb [Lambe], Ann, 58 ; Eliz., 28, 29, 30 ; Isabel, 101 ; John, 28, 29, 30, 31 ; Joseph, 30 ; Richard, 30, 75 ; William, 29, 30, 31, 75.
Lambert, George, 6 ; Guy Lenox, 110 ; Joseph, 58 ; Pamela, 46 ; Phœbe, 46 ; Sarah, 61 ; William, 46.
Lamle, Trystram, 16.
Lane, Edward Henry, 49 ; George, 61 ; Henry, 49, 67 ; Lucy, 49 ; Mary Ann, 66.
Larke, Margaret, 28, 74 ; Thomas, 73 ; William, 28, 73.
Larter, Eliz., 57.
Laughter, Martha, 52.
Lay, James, 66.
Layson [Laison, Laysone, Layston, Laystone], Ann, 30, 74 ; Eliz., 30 : Hannah, 30, 75 ; Henry, 74 ; John, 31 ; Mary, 30, 74, 75 ; Sarah, 30 ; Thomas, 30, 31, 74, 75 ; William, 30.
Leatherdale [Letherdale], Eliz., 76 ; Thomas, 77.
Lee, Elizabeth, 57.
Le François, Mary Anne, 66.
Leggate, Rachel, 72 ; Robert, 53, 72.
Legge, Maria Arabella, 48.
Lenys, Francis, 25 ; Raynold, 25.
Lessye [Lessy], Alice, 53 ; Raynold, 70 n.
Letton, John, 70 n.
Leveson-Gower, Granville, 29 n.
Levits, Louisa, 67.
Lewes, Eliz., 22 ; Jane, 22 ; John, 22, 70 n. ; Mary, 52 ; Rose, 22.
Lewis, Ann, 31 ; Eliz., 31.
Lilbourn, Francis, 55.
Lillie [Lilly], Andrew, 73 n. ; Eliz., 73 n. ; Frances, 54 ; Henery, 55 ; Robert, 57.
Linder, Rhoda, 65.
Lines [Limes, Loins], Ann, 81, 92, 95 ; Anna Maria, 41 ; Eliz., 38, 39, 40, 41, 42, 43, 44, 65, 78, 80, 95 ; Emily, 66, 96 ; Emily Charlotte, 42 ; John, 41, 67 ; Marianne, 38 ; Mary, 65, 80 ; Mary Ann, 42, 43 ; Robert, 43, 80 ; Sarah, 38, 43, 44, 45, 46, 65 ; Thomas, 38, 39, 40, 41, 42, 64, 78, 79, 81, 95 ; William, 39, 40, 78, 95.
Little, John, 48 ; Mary Anne, 48.
Litton, John, 71.
Lodge, John, 74.

ADDENDA ET CORRIGENDA.

Page   9, line 9, for 22 July 1722, read 12 July 1722.
,,   30, ,,   8, after sonne of, insert John and.
..   35, ,,   9. for Mitcham, read Hitcham.
..   43, ,,   36, for Appletons, read Appleton.
..   49, ..   20, for Samuel daughter of. read Samuel son of.
,.   51. ,,   41, for Mary Ann (late Gibbs), read Mary (late Gibbs).
..   57. ,,   30, for Hannau, read Hannah.
,,   80, ..   29, after only daughter, insert of Henry Bence Bence and Elizabeth
                   Susanna his wife.
..   85, ..   46, for Latior, read Lætior.
..   58. 1725, Sept. 9. a note is made of the first mention of marriage by licence.
                This is wrong. The first mention is 1593, May 18.
..   92, line 2, for p. 95, read p. 96.
..   102. The Registers of Aldeburgh from 1600 to 1691 have been lost for some years.
..   103, line 26, should read—
               1792. Dec. 28. Mary Bence, maiden lady, daughter of Robert Bence. Esq.,
                   and Mary his wife (late Eacherd, spinster), aged 83 years.
     103. To Carleton Registers add—

Baptisms.

1622. Oct. 3. John Bence. son of Mr. Alexander Bence and An his wife.
1625. May 11. Alexander Bence, son of Alexander Bence and An his wife.

Marriage.

1707. Oct. 2. Thomas Bence of Kelsale and Margaret Barker of Saxmundham,
               both single.

London: Mitchell and Hughes, Printers, 140 Wardour Street, W.

Genealogy of the Ancient Family of Dener

of Alburgh, Ringsfield, Bexhall, Thorington, etc., all in the County of Suffolk.

www.ingramcontent.com/pod-product-compliance
Lightning Source LLC
Chambersburg PA
CBHW030610270326
41927CB00007B/1114